KT-380-304

good kitchen magic

good kitchen magic

back-to-basics
Cooking
in a flash

carol tennant

MQP

Published by **MQ Publications Limited**
12 The Ivories
6-8 Northampton Street
London N1 2HY
Tel: +44 (0)20 7359 2244
Fax: +44 (0)20 7359 1616
email: mail@mqpublications.com
website: www.mqpublications.com

EDITOR: **Ljljiana Baird**
ILLUSTRATION: **gerardgraphics.co.uk**
DESIGN: **Balley Design Associates**

ISBN: 1-84072-452-8

1 3 5 7 9 8 6 4 2

Printed and bound in China

Contents

The cooking and sharing of a meal with family or friends is one of life's great pleasures. And in our efforts to impress we seek out new and exotic ingredients to make more and more elaborate dishes. Bookshelves groan under the weight of the latest TV tie-ins featuring celebrity chefs, and their recipes can often lead to disappointment when we fail to 'throw together a delicious meal with the minimum fuss'.

But are we losing track of what is important? Yes, cooking is an art form, but it is based on a series of basic techniques that we then build on. In the not so distant past, the majority of these basic techniques were

Introduction

passed down from grandmother to mother to daughter. In our fast paced, multi-tasking age of equality, this link has been broken. Many of us will turn our hand to an exotic chicken curry, but may not know the correct way to roast a pork joint with crispy crackling or cook perfect rice.

The aim of this book is to take you through those basic cookery techniques that will provide the stepping stones for you to move on and cook more advanced dishes. With the help of this book, you can gain the confidence to prepare traditional stuffed roast chicken with all the trimmings, to poach salmon, to bake wholemeal bread, and shortcrust pastry. And for anyone who usually reaches for the jars or bottles, there are recipes for a whole range of classic and popular sauces, such as apple, mint, tomato, and pesto. Also included are some more unusual dishes, such as fennel and cilantro (coriander) salad, and pasta and bean soup. Together, these recipes will provide a good repertoire of dishes for anyone interested in learning to cook successfully or improving their skills.

Mastering the basics also allows you to take shortcuts—for example, if you can already make mayonnaise by hand, and can understand the basic method, you wil be better equipped to know what to do if something goes wrong when you are making it using a food processor.

Throughout the book, there are helpful tips, such as how to blind bake or make a bouquet garni, as well as rescue remedies to save the day when things go off course. Many of the recipes have variations that will allow you to expand your range gradually.

Cooking doesn't have to be complicated to impress. A simple, tasty, nutritious recipe prepared the correct way, and cooked at the right temperature for the right amount of time, will be praised and remembered long after the wine and conversation have dried up.

Poultry

What could be more appealing than a perfectly roasted chicken with stuffing and gravy and all the accompaniments? Or a fine Christmas turkey with all the trimmings? Poultry is a versatile and delicious meat that lends itself to a wide variety of dishes, from the traditional to the modern.

Chicken

Chicken is an excellent source of first-class protein and, without its skin, is also a relatively low-fat meat. It suits many methods of cooking, including roasting, frying, broiling, barbecuing and braising, but should not be overcooked as it can dry out. It also goes with a huge variety of flavors and is found in most world cuisines—from Indian and Chinese to Moroccan and Thai.

Superstores and butchers now stock a wide range of birds, both fresh and frozen, which vary according to the method of rearing. The three main types of bird are:

- **Intensively reared (broiling) hens** (often simply labeled 'fresh')
- **Free range**
- **Organic**

Fresh chickens

Intensively farmed or battery chickens are often labeled as 'fresh', which simply means that the bird has not been frozen. These will be the cheapest to buy. Birds are kept indoors in

Roasting times for poultry

Type of bird	Cooking time—minutes per lb/kilo
Chicken	25 minutes per 1lb 2oz/500g plus another 20 minutes if necessary @ 375° F/Gas 5/190° C.
Turkey	30–40 minutes @ 425° F/Gas 7/220° C, then 20 minutes per 1lb 2oz/500g @ 350° F/Gas 4/180° C.
Poussin	40–45 minutes @ 400° F/Gas 6/200° C.
Duck	20 minutes @ 425° F/Gas 7/220° C, then 30 minutes per 1lb 2oz/500g @ 350° F/Gas 4/180° C.
Goose	30 minutes @ 425° F/Gas 7/220° C, then 20 minutes per 1lb 2oz/500g @ 350° F/Gas 4/180° C.

confined spaces with little room for movement. They are routinely given growth enhancers, as well as antibiotics to prevent them developing infections, which would spread quickly in such conditions. They are bred for rapid growth and as a result are found to have skeletal and heart defects. These chickens usually have a life span of less than 50 days.

Most store-bought chickens are broiling hens, which have been bred mainly for their meat rather than for egg production. Also available are poussins, or spring chickens (which are also sometimes called Cornish hens). These are very young chickens —battery-reared poussins will be slaughtered as young as 4 weeks.

Traditional Stuffed Roast Chicken

SERVES 4

5oz/150g sliced white bread, crusts removed

4 tablespoons/2oz/50g butter, softened

1 onion, chopped

1 stalk celery, finely chopped

1 garlic clove, crushed

4oz/115g pork sausagemeat, crumbled

zest of ½ lemon

1 egg, lightly beaten

1 tablespoon chopped fresh sage or 1 teaspoon dried sage or poultry seasoning

½ teaspoon paprika

3lb 5oz/1.5kg chicken

salt and freshly ground black pepper

Preheat the oven to 425° F/Gas 7/220° C.

❶ Cut the bread into ½in/1cm cubes and put into a large bowl. Set aside.

❷ Melt 2 tablespoons/1oz/25g of the butter in a frying pan over a medium heat until foaming. Add the onion and celery and cook for 5–7 minutes until softened and translucent. Add the garlic and cook for a further minute. Add the sausagemeat. Increase the heat and cook for a further 5 minutes, stirring once or twice only, until the sausagemeat is browned and cooked through. Remove any excess fat that may have come from the sausagemeat with a metal spoon and discard.

❸ Add the sausagemeat mixture, lemon zest, egg, sage, and paprika to the bread. Season well and mix together thoroughly—you may find your hands are best for this.

❹ Wash the chicken inside and out and dry with paper towel. Turn the bird so that the wings are nearest you with the breast uppermost. Take a handful of the stuffing mixture and put it under the flap of skin between the wings—you'll probably fit two handfuls. Press in well, then pull the skin down to cover the stuffing. Using poultry skewers or cocktail sticks, secure the skin underneath the bird. Take the remaining stuffing and use to stuff the body cavity.

❺ Smear the breast and legs of the chicken with the remaining butter. Season well with salt and freshly ground black pepper.

❻ Calculate the cooking time according to the Roasting Times chart on page 8. Put the chicken into a roasting pan and cook for the calculated time, reducing the oven temperature to 375° F/Gas 5/190° C after the first 20 minutes. Every 20 minutes or so, carefully baste the bird with the juices in the pan.

❼ To check if the bird is cooked, remove it from the oven. Using a skewer or small sharp knife, pierce the bird in the thickest part of the thigh. If the juices run clear, without a trace of pink, the bird is cooked. Also, gently pull the leg away from the body. If it gives easily, the bird is cooked.

8 Transfer the bird to a carving board and let rest for at least 10 minutes. Remove the stuffing from the body cavity and transfer to a serving dish. Keep warm. Carve the bird and serve with gravy (see below).

Stuffing variations

Add 1 peeled, chopped apple and ¹/₂ cup/1oz/25g of chopped walnuts to the bread along with the sausagemeat mixture. Cook 1¹/₄ cups/8oz/225g of mixed long-grain and wild rice according to the packet instructions until tender. Add 4 chopped green (spring) onions, 1 shredded carrot, 1 cup/4oz/125g of sliced mushrooms, 1 crushed garlic clove, 2 tablespoons of soy sauce, 1 tablespoon of honey, 1 tablespoon of vegetable oil and mix well. Use to stuff the bird and cook as above.

Gravy

After transferring the bird to a carving board, remove as much fat as possible from the roasting pan. Tilt the pan so that all the juices collect in one corner and, using a large metal spoon, skim the fat off the top and discard. Put the pan over a medium heat. Add about 2 teaspoons of all-purpose or plain flour and whisk well until smooth. Gradually add ¹/₂ cup/4fl oz/125ml of red or white wine. Bring to the boil and simmer gently for 2–3 minutes until thickened. Gradually add 1¹/₄ cups/10fl oz/300ml of chicken stock (see page 14), or a combination of chicken stock and the cooking water from the vegetables or potatoes. Whisk until smooth. Bring to the boil and simmer for 5–7 minutes until thickened and reduced. Taste for seasoning. Simmer for a further few minutes to reduce if the flavor is weak. Taste again and add seasoning as necessary.

Why rest the bird after cooking?

Resting meat before carving allows any juices that have accumulated under the skin to seep back into the meat, keeping it succulent and making carving easier. This is true for all roasted meats.

Carving

The most important asset when carving a bird is a sharp knife. A carving fork is useful, but not essential. To carve the bird, first remove the legs and wings (do this by pulling them off—they will come away easily). Slice the meat from the legs, if preferred, or serve them whole on the bone. Turn the bird so that the wing end is nearest you, but so that the bird is at a slight angle to you (if you are right-handed, angle the bird so that the breast on the right is nearest you or vice versa if left-handed). Secure the bird using a carving fork in the breast furthest from you and slice the meat off the breast. Alternatively, remove the breast meat entirely by slicing along the back bone and then cutting the breast meat on the carving board.

Flavoring under the skin

As well as using stuffing, chickens can be flavored under the skin. For all flavorings, first carefully work your fingers up under the skin over the breast and legs to create pockets, taking care not to tear the skin.

Thinly slice about 3½ oz/100g of chorizo sausage. Lay the slices under the skin over the legs and breasts.

Mix together 4 tablespoons/2oz/50g of softened butter with 1 tablespoon of chopped fresh thyme leaves, 1 crushed garlic clove, the finely grated zest of 1 orange and plenty of salt and freshly ground black pepper. Spread this mixture over the legs and breast meat under the skin.

Simplest of all, put sprigs of fresh thyme, sage, rosemary, and parsley under the skin. Season the skin well before roasting.

Basic Chicken Stock

MAKES 1.325 QUARTS/2¼ PINTS/1.25 LITERS

1 large carrot, scrubbed and trimmed
1 large onion, skin on
(this will add color to the stock)
2 celery stalks, trimmed
carcass from a roasted chicken

1 bay leaf
1 leafy sprig fresh thyme
6 black peppercorns
approximately 1.6 quarts/2¾ pints/
1.5 liters cold water

❶ Chop the carrot into large chunks, halve the onion lengthwise through the root, and chop the celery into large chunks. Put into a large pan with the chicken carcass, bay leaf, thyme, and peppercorns. Pour over the water, ensuring that there is enough to cover the carcass. Bring slowly to the boil. As the water comes up to simmering point, a scum will rise to the surface—this should be removed with a metal spoon and discarded.

❷ Once the water comes up to the boil, reduce the heat so that the surface of the liquid barely moves—this will keep the stock from becoming cloudy. The pan can be partially covered at this stage and the stock allowed to bubble gently for about 2 hours.

❸ After 2 hours, taste the stock. You may need to reduce it to concentrate the flavor (see opposite). Once you are happy with the flavor, strain the stock by setting a colander over a large bowl or saucepan. Pour the stock into the colander along with the carcass and vegetables. Let drain until all the liquid has drained off into the bowl or saucepan, then discard the carcass and vegetables. Add salt to the stock to taste.

How do I make a bouquet garni?

Bouquet garni can be bought ready-made in little sachets, but they are very easy to make fresh. Take 2 pieces of celery, each about 3in/7.5cm long. On 1 piece of celery, lay a bay leaf, a sprig of fresh thyme, a garlic clove and a few black peppercorns. Top with the second piece of celery and tie securely with kitchen string. Add to soups, stocks, or sauces and remove before serving.

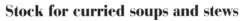

Stock for curried soups and stews

Leave out the bay leaf and thyme from the basic stock recipe and add a small bunch of chopped fresh cilantro (coriander), 2 thin slices of ginger (don't worry about peeling the ginger) and a couple of cloves of peeled garlic.

Stock for Chinese dishes

Leave out the bay leaf and thyme from the basic stock recipe and add 2 cloves of peeled garlic, 2 thin slices of ginger, 3 roughly chopped green (spring) onions, 1 star anise and half a cinnamon stick.

Pilafs and Persian-style soups and stews

Leave out the thyme from the basic stock recipe and add 2 cloves of peeled garlic, 6 cloves, 5 crushed cardamom pods, half a cinnamon stick, and a small pinch of saffron. This stock has a lovely pale yellow color and wonderful fragrance.

Reducing stock

If you want to reduce your stock to make a richly flavored base for a sauce, allow it to simmer until the volume is reduced, usually by about half, or, if necessary, until only a little remains and the consistency is syrupy. At this stage other flavorings, such as cream or crème fraîche, may be added, or the sauce can also be finished with a little butter.

Storing stock

Keep the stock covered in the refrigerator. If it isn't used within 3 days, return it to a saucepan and bring to the boil. Boil hard for 2 minutes, let cool and return to the refrigerator for up to a further 3 days.

Why not use a cube?

Stock cubes tend to have a lot of additional ingredients in them, which can make all your soups and sauces taste the same. Fresh stock has a much more subtle flavor, which doesn't mask flavors from other ingredients, and it is virtually effortless to make, requiring just a little chopping. Use cubes only as a quick standby.

When using the stock in a recipe, ensure that it comes up to boiling point and let boil for at least 2 minutes.

Alternatively, stock can be frozen. Smaller quantities are often useful, so freeze stock in containers that hold about 1¼ cups/ 10fl oz/300ml (you can always defrost more than one).

Another useful tip is to freeze stock in ice cube trays and then transfer the cubes to a re-sealable bag. Cubes can be added straight to sauces without the need to defrost first. Frozen stock can be kept for up to one month. As with all frozen food, label containers with the date the stock was frozen to ensure you use it in good time.

"...and what about these tasty variations"

Stocks are useful additions to a wide range of recipes. In risotto, and other rice dishes such as pilafs, cooking the rice in stock is vital or the finished dish will be bland. It is also useful to bear in mind what the stock will be used for and add different flavorings accordingly.

Coq au Vin

SERVES 6–8

5lb/2.2kg chicken (or 2 smaller chickens)
3 tablespoons/2fl oz/45ml olive oil
2 cups/9oz/250g baby onions or shallots,
  peeled and halved if large
³/₄ cup/3¹/₂ oz/100g smoked bacon
  or pancetta, cut into lardons,
    or roughly chopped
2 large bushy sprigs fresh thyme

2 bay leaves
3 cups/1¹/₄ pints/750ml red wine
2 cups/8oz/225g small open
  cap mushrooms
2 tablespoons all-purpose or plain flour
2 tablespoons/1oz/25g butter, softened
salt and freshly ground black pepper

Preheat the oven to 275° F/Gas 1/140° C.

❶ First, joint the chicken. Using a large sharp knife or poultry shears, cut along either side of the backbone and remove. Now remove the legs by inserting the knife or shears at the joint with the body. Cut each leg in two. Split the breastbone in two then cut each breast crosswise into two pieces, one piece to have the wing attached. You should end up with eight pieces.

❷ Heat the oil over a medium-high heat in a large ovenproof casserole dish. Add the chicken pieces, skin-side-down, in batches if necessary. Cook until browned on both sides, then remove to a plate. Remove any excess fat from the pan, leaving about 2 tablespoons.

❸ Reduce the heat and add the onions or shallots and bacon. Cook for 5–7 minutes until well-browned and the bacon is crisp. Return the chicken to the pan along with the thyme

and bay leaves. Now add the red wine, stirring well to scrape up any brown bits clinging to the bottom of the pan. Add a little black pepper. Bring to the boil and reduce the heat to a simmer. Cover the casserole and transfer to the lower part of the oven. Cook for 1¹/₂ hours, then add the mushrooms. Stir well and return to the oven for a further 30–45 minutes until the mushrooms are tender.

❹ Remove from the oven. Taste the sauce. If necessary, bring to the boil on the hob and simmer until the flavor is more concentrated. Meanwhile, mix together the flour and butter to a smooth paste. Add the paste, a little at a time, to the sauce, stirring well, until the sauce has thickened enough to coat a spoon. Season to taste. You may not need all of the paste. Serve with mashed potatoes.

❺ This casserole is very good if made a day ahead and refrigerated overnight, allowing the flavors to develop. Reheat well before serving.

"What can I do with the leftovers?"

This recipe uses fresh chicken stock, thereby making the most of the whole chicken. Always be sure not to store cooked meat on the bone. Strip the carcass and store the meat separately in the refrigerator.

Chicken and Pearl Barley Soup

SERVES 4

1 quart/1¾ pints/1 liter chicken stock
1 cup/7oz/200g pearl barley
2 cups/12oz/350g leftover chicken, roughly chopped

3 tablespoons fresh parsley, chopped
salt and freshly ground black pepper

❶ Bring the stock to the boil, then add the pearl barley. Reduce the heat to a gentle simmer. Cover and cook for 45 minutes to 1 hour until the pearl barley is tender and swollen.

❷ Add the chicken meat and simmer for a further 5 minutes until heated through. Add the parsley, season to taste and serve immediately.

Crispy Oven-baked Chicken Wings with Potato Wedges

SERVES 4

2lb 4oz/1kg chicken wings
3 tablespoons all-purpose or plain flour
1/2 teaspoon ground cayenne pepper
1 teaspoon paprika
1 teaspoon dried oregano

1 tablespoon olive oil
1 garlic clove, crushed
4 large potatoes
salt and freshly ground black pepper

Preheat the oven to 400° F/Gas 6/200° C.

❶ Trim the wings by removing the wing tip. If you prefer, cut the wings in two at the joint.

❷ Put the flour, cayenne pepper, paprika, oregano, and plenty of salt and pepper into a large, clear plastic bag (a freezer bag is ideal). Shake well to mix, then add the chicken wings. Close the bag tightly at the top and shake until all the wings are well coated in the flour mixture. Transfer the wings to a baking sheet, shaking any excess flour back into the bag. Discard any unused mixture.

❸ For the potatoes, in a large bowl, mix together the olive oil, garlic, and plenty of salt and pepper. Cut each potato into eight wedges and add to the bowl. Toss well to mix. Transfer the potatoes to a baking sheet.

❹ Bake the wings toward the top of the oven for 30 minutes until golden and crisp. Bake the potato wedges on the shelf below the wings, turning once during cooking.

❺ Drain the wings and potatoes on paper towel before serving with ready-made barbecue sauce or sweet chili sauce for dipping.

Duck and goose

Superstores now have farmed ducks available most of the year round, and at a reasonable price. You can usually choose from duck or duckling and between different types of duck, for example Barbary. Butchers will have wild ducks available in season. The flavor of a wild duck is, as you would imagine, gamier and stronger. They are also less fatty. Geese are not so readily available, except at Christmas when they are traditionally served.

Look for a duck or goose with a good, even shape and dry skin. Wetness can indicate that the bird has been frozen or partially frozen.

What can I do with goose fat?

Geese will often be sold with a separate bag of fat that has been removed by the butcher. Do not throw this away—it is excellent for use in cooking, especially when roasting or frying potatoes. To render this fat, put it into a large pan and cover with water. Bring slowly to the boil. Simmer until the fat has melted and the water has evaporated. Let the fat cool, then decant into small containers. Freeze until needed or use within 7–10 days. Use in place of oil in cooking.

Flavors to accompany duck

Since duck and geese are very fatty birds, mainly under the skin, they are both best served with slightly astringent, yet sweet, flavors. Classically, roast duck is served with an orange or cherry sauce but it also goes very well with currants.

Goose is also delicious served with gooseberries, and goes particularly well with prunes.

Roasting duck and goose

When roasting a duck or goose, be sure to first dry the skin well. Then using a fork or skewer, prick the skin, taking care not to pierce the flesh. This will help the fat to escape during cooking. Sprinkle the skin well with salt, which will help to draw out any excess moisture and leave a crispy finish. Set the bird on a rack in the roasting pan. You may need to remove the fat during cooking.

Duck giblet stock

Ducks are too fatty to make stock with, but if you're going to make gravy or a sauce requiring stock for your duck, giblet stock is very easy. Wash and dry the giblets (which usually come in a bag inside the duck). Put into a medium saucepan along with a halved onion, a roughly chopped carrot, a roughly chopped celery stalk, a peeled garlic clove, a few black peppercorns, a sprig of fresh thyme or parsley and a bay leaf. Cover with water and bring slowly to the boil. Simmer, covered, for 1½ hours. Strain and use as necessary.

Seared Duck Breasts with Orange Sauce

SERVES 4

2 large duck breasts
1 shallot, chopped
1 garlic clove, chopped
1 tablespoon fresh thyme leaves
2 tablespoons Cointreau or
orange-flavored liqueur

2 tablespoons port
¼ cup/2fl oz/50ml chicken stock
finely grated zest and juice of 1 orange
2 tablespoons orange marmalade
salt and freshly ground black pepper

❶ To prepare the duck breasts, lightly score the skin at ½in/1cm intervals. Now turn the duck breasts and repeat to give a diamond pattern. Be careful not to cut the flesh. These cuts will allow the fat to escape.

❷ Heat a large frying pan over a medium-high heat. When hot, add the duck breasts, skin-side-down. Reduce the heat to medium and cook for about 7–8 minutes until well browned. Turn and cook for a further 3–4 minutes. Remove from the pan.

❸ Remove as much fat as possible from the pan with a metal spoon, leaving about 1 tablespoon only. Return the pan to a medium heat and add the shallot. Cook for 3–4 minutes until softened, then add the garlic and thyme. Cook for a further 1 minute before adding the Cointreau and port. Simmer until reduced by half. Add the chicken stock,

orange juice and zest and bring to the boil. Simmer until reduced by half. Stir in the marmalade until melted. Season to taste.

❹ Slice the duck breasts thickly and serve immediately with the sauce.

...with cherry sauce

Cook the duck breasts as directed above. Make a sauce by simmering together 1½ cups/5oz/150g of good quality Morello cherry jam, ½ cup/5fl oz/ 150ml of red wine and 2 tablespoons of port for 10 minutes until thickened.

Turkey

Turkeys come in a range of sizes, from about 9lb/4kg up to 25lb/11.5kg or more. As a rule of thumb, allow about 1lb 2oz/500g per person when calculating the size of turkey you will need.

The timings and quantities in the recipe overleaf are for a 10–12lb/4.5–5.5kg turkey. The Roasting Times chart on page 8 will help you to calculate cooking times for birds of different weights.

The stuffing in the recipe is cooked separately, so that the bird can cook through more quickly. This will help to avoid overcooking and drying out. You could also use the stuffing from Traditional Stuffed Roast Chicken (see page 10)—just ensure that you double the quantities.

Turkey carcass stock

Follow the method and ingredients for the chicken stock on page 14, adding an extra carrot, onion, and celery stalk and increasing the water as necessary to cover all the contents of the pan. You may need to break or chop the carcass to make it fit into the pan.

I CAN'T WAIT FOR TURKEY TIME!

Roast Turkey with all the Trimmings

10–12lb/4.5–5.5kg turkey, thawed if frozen *(see below)*

1 onion, halved

handful fresh thyme sprigs

3 bay leaves

1 lemon, halved

6 tablespoons/3oz/75g butter, softened

6–8 rashers smoked streaky bacon

2 tablespoons all-purpose or plain flour *(optional)*

salt and freshly ground black pepper

FOR THE STUFFING

2 tablespoons/1oz/25g butter

1 onion, finely chopped

1 celery stalk, finely chopped

1 garlic clove, crushed

8oz/225g good quality pork and herb sausagemeat, crumbled

1 large cooking apple, cored and roughly chopped

$\frac{1}{2}$ cup/2oz/50g chestnuts, roughly chopped

8oz/225g sliced white bread, crust removed and cubed

zest of 1 lemon

1 large egg, lightly beaten

1 tablespoon fresh thyme leaves, or 1 teaspoon dried thyme

1 tablespoon fresh sage, chopped, or 1 teaspoon dried sage

2 teaspoons fresh rosemary, chopped, or $\frac{1}{2}$ teaspoon dried rosemary

1 tablespoon fresh parsley, chopped

❶ If your turkey is frozen, allow time for the bird to thaw—it is essential that there is no ice inside the bird. For a 10–12lb/4.5–5.5kg turkey allow at least 36 hours. Put the bird on the lowest shelf of the refrigerator on a tray. Remove the defrosted turkey the night before cooking to let it come to room temperature. About half an hour before cooking, preheat the oven to 400° F/Gas 6/200° C.

❷ To make the stuffing, melt the butter over a medium heat in a large frying pan until foaming. Add the onion and celery and cook for 5–7 minutes until softened but not brown. Add the garlic and cook for a further 30 seconds or so. Now increase the heat to medium-high and add the sausagemeat. Cook for a further 7–8 minutes until browned. Tip into a large bowl.

❸ Add the apple, chestnuts, bread, lemon zest, egg, thyme, sage, rosemary, and parsley. Add plenty of salt and freshly ground black pepper. Mix well until everything is coated in egg.

❹ Season the turkey well inside the body cavity. Put the bird on the worktop with the wings nearest you. Lift the flap of skin and put 2 or 3 good handfuls of the stuffing underneath this flap. You might be able to fit another handful. Press it in well, then cover with the flap of skin. Secure the flap of skin under the bird using cocktail sticks or skewers. Transfer the remaining stuffing mixture to an ovenproof dish—a small lasagna dish is ideal. Set aside.

5 Put the onion halves, thyme sprigs, bay leaves, and lemon halves inside the cavity. Smear the skin on the breast and legs with the softened butter. Season well. Lay the bacon across the breast meat—you can lattice the strips together first or simply lay them neatly in rows, if you like.

6 Tear off two long strips of double width aluminum foil. They should be about 3 times the length of the roasting pan. Lay one sheet lengthwise along the pan and the other crosswise, to form a cross. Put the turkey in the center of the foil. Fold up the foil over the bird, leaving a large space, then fold the other section of foil to completely enclose it.

7 Transfer to a large roasting pan and place on the lowest shelf of the oven. Cook for 30 minutes. Reduce the temperature to 350° F/Gas 4/180° C and cook for a further 3 hours, opening the foil and folding it right back for the last 30 minutes to crisp the skin. At this time, put the separate stuffing mixture in the oven on a shelf above the turkey. Cook the stuffing for 30 minutes.

8 Once the cooking time is up, use three tests to check that the bird is cooked. Pierce the flesh in the thickest part of the thigh to see if the juices run clear. Tug on a leg, to test if it comes away from the body easily. Finally, tip the bird up and check that the juices inside are clear. If the bird fails any of these tests, return it to the oven for a further 15 minutes and test again.

9 Transfer the bird to a large carving board. Remove the bacon and set aside. The bird needs to rest for at least 20–30 minutes before carving. Tip the juices from the foil into the pan and scrape up any meat residue. Skim off any excess fat, leaving 1–2 tablespoons.

10 To make the gravy, put the roasting pan over medium heat. Pour in the giblet stock (see page 27) and about 1 scant cup/ 7fl oz/200ml of water. Bring to the boil and simmer until reduced by about one third. Taste, and if the flavor is concentrated enough, season. If the flavor needs more concentrating, carry on simmering until reduced by half and taste again.

11 If you prefer a thicker gravy, mix together the flour with about 4 tablespoons of cold water. Whisk this mixture, a little at a time, into the simmering gravy until you are happy with the thickness. You may not need all the flour and water mixture.

12 Carve the bird for serving and transfer the sliced meat to a large serving platter. Serve with the gravy and bacon.

Giblet stock

Whether the turkey is fresh or frozen, it will arrive with a bag of giblets inside the body cavity. Remove these as soon as possible—when you get it home with a fresh bird and as soon as it is thawed with a frozen bird. Keep them separately in the refrigerator. A well-flavored giblet stock is essential for Christmas-day gravy. Wash the giblets and trim them of any fat. Put into a medium saucepan with a halved onion, a chopped carrot, a chopped celery stalk, a sprig of thyme, a bay leaf and a few peppercorns. Cover with cold water and bring slowly to the boil. Skim off any scum that rises to the surface. Cover, and simmer very gently for 1½ hours. Strain and set aside until needed.

Roast potatoes

For the best roast potatoes, peel about 8–12oz/225–350g potatoes per person. Cut into large chunks. Put into cold, salted water and bring to the boil. Cook for 7 minutes, then drain well. Return the potatoes to the saucepan and pop on the lid. Shake the pan so that the outer layer of potato becomes very rough.

Meanwhile, put a shallow roasting tray big enough to hold all the potatoes in a single layer into the oven with about a ¼in/5mm layer of vegetable oil (or better still, vegetable oil and goose fat) above the turkey (or on a high shelf).

When the oil is hot, remove the tray from the oven and carefully transfer the potatoes to the tray using tongs. Turn the potatoes in the oil to lightly coat them. Return the tray to the oven and cook the potatoes for 30–40 minutes until golden on the bottom. Turn the potatoes and continue to cook for a further 30 minutes. Drain on paper towel before serving hot.

Cranberry, orange and sage sauce

Cranberries are a classic accompaniment to roast turkey. Put 3 cups/12oz/350g of cranberries into a medium saucepan with 1 onion, which has been finely grated, 3 tablespoons of brown sugar and the juice and zest of 1 orange. Bring to the boil and simmer very gently, stirring often, until the cranberries have softened. Stir in 1 tablespoon of finely chopped fresh sage and simmer for 5 minutes. Stir in 2–3 tablespoons of port and remove from the heat. Season well. Serve warm or cold.

Gravy tips

For a richer gravy than the one described in the main recipe, add ½ cup/4fl oz/120ml of red or white wine to the roasting pan and let reduce until syrupy before adding the giblet stock and water.

Meat

Current health advice suggests that we should eat less meat in our day-to-day diets, yet today's farming practices, which ensure that meat prices are kept low, encourage us to include more meat in our diets. The answer lies, perhaps, in spending a bit more on good quality meat that has been less intensively reared, but buying it less often. In this way, we will reduce our meat consumption while providing ourselves with a much better quality meal when we do buy it.

Inexperienced cooks often find meat cookery daunting and can be discouraged from even attempting a simple roast meal. The secret is to choose the correct cut of meat for the method of cooking and follow some simple guidelines as provided below.

Roasting

Roasting is a cooking method that involves exposing a whole joint to an even heat in an oven. You should begin roasting at a high temperature in order to seal the outside of the meat and give it a tasty caramelized crust. Then, lower the temperature to ensure that the meat cooks evenly all the way through.

Pot roasting involves the long, slow cooking of a (usually) cheaper cut of meat in a pot with a little liquid and perhaps some vegetables. This creates a steamy atmosphere in which the meat can cook without losing any

Roasting times for joints of meat

Type of meat	Cooking time—minutes per lb/kilo, bone-in/boneless
Lamb	30 minutes @ 450° F/Gas 8/230° C, then 350° F/Gas 4/180° C for 35 minutes per 1lb 2oz/500g for rare. Add 5 minutes per 1lb 2oz/500g for medium and 10 minutes per 1lb 2oz/500g for well done.
Beef	20 minutes @ 475° F/Gas 9/250° C, then 375° F/Gas 5/190° C for 15 minutes per 1lb 2oz/500g for rare. Add 15 extra minutes for medium rare or 30 extra minutes for well done.
Pork	20 minutes @ 475° F/Gas 9/250° C, then 375° F/Gas 5/190° C for 40 minutes per 1lb 2oz/500g for leg or loin. Other cuts lower heat to 350° F/Gas 4/180° C and cook for 50 minutes per 1lb 2 oz/500g.

How do I get crispy crackling on my roast pork?

Unwrap your pork joint as soon as you get it home. It is very important that you dry the joint carefully with paper towel first—a wet rind will never become crispy when it is cooked.

If possible, leave the pork uncovered in the refrigerator until you are ready to cook it—this should be no more than a day, however—which will help to dry the joint further as well.

Using a very sharp knife or craft knife, score the skin of the pork joint at about $1/4$in/5mm intervals all over. Your butcher can also do this for you if you ask. Just before cooking, give the skin a generous sprinkling of salt all over and do not add any fat. Use a shallow roasting pan to ensure that the crackling gets a good blast of the heat.

An interesting way to add even more flavor to your roast is to make slits in the meat using a small, sharp knife and insert slices of garlic and sprigs of fresh sage, thyme, or rosemary before roasting.

moisture. The meat can also be marinated first to impart even more flavor. The resulting cooked joint will be very moist and tender.

Cuts for oven roasting

As a general rule, it is best to roast leaner cuts of meat, such as beef sirloin, loin of pork, pork tenderloin, leg or shoulder of lamb, and if possible, roast them on the bone. The bone helps to conduct heat to the center of the meat and also holds the meat together for carving. However, these cuts are also available boned and rolled, and can be successfully stuffed and roasted or simply rolled and roasted.

Cuts for pot-roasting

Beef is the most popular meat for pot-roasting, although ham and bacon joints can also be cooked successfully this way. Choose top rump, chuck, blade or brisket for beef pot-roasting. Bacon collar, middle-cut gammon, corner gammon and gammon slipper are all suitable joints of ham for pot-roasting or for a combination of pot-roasting and roasting.

Roast Leg of Lamb

SERVES 6–8

1 leg of lamb	1 cup/8fl oz/250ml red wine
(weigh once prepared for cooking)	1¼ cups/10fl oz/300ml lamb stock
2–3 garlic cloves, sliced	or water
2–3 sprigs fresh rosemary	salt and freshly ground black pepper

Preheat the oven to 425° F/Gas 7/220° C.

❶ Calculate the total cooking time using the Roasting Times chart on page 28, first determining whether you want the meat rare, medium or well done.

❷ Using a small, sharp knife, make about 8–10 deep incisions in the meat. Into each incision, insert a slice of garlic along with a few leaves of rosemary (you can usually pull off small bunches of leaves attached at the stem end). Season the lamb well all over with salt and pepper. Transfer to a large roasting pan.

❸ Cook according to the chart and your calculations. When finished, remove the meat from the roasting pan to a carving board. Let rest for 10–15 minutes.

❹ To make the gravy, remove as much fat as possible from the roasting pan, using a metal spoon. Place the pan over a medium heat. When sizzling, pour in the red wine. Using a spoon or whisk, scrape up any residue in the bottom of the pan. Allow the wine to simmer rapidly until reduced to a syrupy consistency.

Now add the stock or water (if you have any water from cooking vegetables or potatoes, use that). Bring to the boil and simmer rapidly until reduced by about half. Taste, and add a little seasoning. If the flavor is not concentrated enough, continue reducing a little more. Strain the gravy into a jug or gravy boat.

❺ Slice the meat and serve with the gravy.

What is deglazing?

Deglazing is the common term used in recipes to refer to adding liquid to a saucepan or roasting pan. The liquid is used to lift the browned bits from the bottom of the pan so that they flavor the resulting sauce or gravy.

Classic sauces to accompany roasts

Apple sauce

This is a traditional accompaniment to roast pork. Using 1 apple per serving (a cooking apple will give a smooth apple sauce, while an eating apple will stay firmer and have more texture when cooked), peel, core and roughly chop into a saucepan. Add 2 tablespoons of water and about 2 teaspoons of lemon juice per apple. Cover and bring to the boil. Reduce the heat and cook gently for about 10 minutes until soft enough to mash with a fork. Add a little sugar to taste and serve. The sauce is also delicious with herby pork sausages.

Mint sauce

This is a simple accompaniment to roast lamb. Mix together 4 tablespoons of finely chopped fresh mint with 2 tablespoons of white wine vinegar and 2 tablespoons of water. Season with a little salt and serve.

Basic meat gravy

The principle of making gravy applies to all roasted meats. Remove the roast from the pan. Spoon off any excess fat, leaving about 1 tablespoon, and discard. Put the pan over a medium heat and add about a glassful of red or white wine. Simmer rapidly, stirring to scrape up any residue in the pan, until reduced and syrupy. Now add about 1¼ cups/10fl oz/300ml of meat or chicken stock.

Bring to the boil and simmer rapidly until reduced by about one third. If you prefer a thicker stock, mix together 1 tablespoon of all-purpose or plain flour with 3 tablespoons of cold water to make a smooth paste. Gradually add this mixture to the boiling gravy, whisking well, until the mixture thickens to taste. Strain if you prefer a smooth gravy and season to taste.

Creamed horseradish

This sauce is excellent served with roast beef. Lightly whip ²⁄₃ cup/5fl oz/150ml plus 1 tablespoon of double cream and add 1–2 tablespoons of grated horseradish to taste (either fresh or from a jar). Season well and serve with hot or cold roast beef. This is also very good served with smoked trout, mackerel, or smoked salmon.

"What can I do with the leftovers?"

Leftover roast lamb is delicious sliced thinly in sandwiches, but can also be used to create quick supper dishes, such as the following recipe.

Lamb or Beef Curry Supper

SERVES 4

2 tablespoons vegetable oil
1 onion, chopped
1in/2.5cm piece fresh ginger, finely grated
1 garlic clove, chopped
1 medium tomato, peeled and roughly chopped
1 teaspoon ground cilantro (coriander)
2 tablespoons curry paste *(mild, medium or hot, to taste)*

²/₃ cup/5fl oz/150ml vegetable or meat stock or water
14oz/400g can chickpeas, drained and rinsed
1½ cups/3½ oz/100g button mushrooms
2 cups/9oz/250g leftover roast lamb or beef, roughly chopped
5 tablespoons Greek yogurt
3 tablespoons fresh cilantro (coriander), chopped
salt and freshly ground black pepper

❶ Heat 1 tablespoon of the oil in a medium saucepan. Add the onion, ginger, and garlic and cook for about 5 minutes until softened. Transfer to a blender or food processor along with the tomato. Process until fairly smooth.

❷ Return to the pan along with the cilantro (coriander), curry paste, stock, and chickpeas. Cover and simmer for 20 minutes.

❸ Meanwhile, heat the rest of the oil in a frying pan and add the mushrooms. Cook over a high heat for 5 minutes until golden.

❹ Add the mushrooms with the meat to the chickpea mixture and simmer for 5 minutes. Remove from the heat and let stand for 1–2 minutes. Add the yogurt and cilantro. Season to taste and serve with basmati rice.

Stewing, braising, and casseroling

These terms are all different names for what is essentially the same cooking method. Meat is cooked in a pot, either flameproof or ovenproof or both, along with some liquid. Generally speaking, stews are cooked on top of the stove and casseroles are cooked in the oven. Braised dishes usually involve bigger pieces of meat, for example a lamb hot-pot generally uses lamb cutlets. Their main advantage is that they can be prepared, and even cooked, ahead with very little attention. They are usually economical, too, as the meat can be stretched with the addition of vegetables and potatoes. Casseroles are also suitable for freezing, so one batch can make more than one meal.

Cuts

Superstores often have packets of meat labeled 'stewing' or 'braising'. These are useful, but do not specify the actual cut of meat you are buying. Beef for stewing should have plenty of connective tissue, and more fat than cuts for roasting. The reason for this is that the connective tissue breaks down during the slow cooking, providing flavor and body to the finished dish. Therefore, cuts from the forequarter (that is, from the waist up), which is the portion of the animal that initiates its movements and therefore has more muscle, are the best cuts. The names for these cuts vary from region to region but are generally shoulder, blade, chuck, flank, and brisket (which needs to be carefully prepared because it has a lot of gristle and fat—ask your butcher

to do this for you). For stewing and casseroling in particular, choose leg, neck or shin. If available, cheek is also excellent.

Cuts of lamb for stewing are middle neck or end of neck. For braising, use best end of neck chops and lamb shanks. Pork for braising, again, usually comes from the region around the shoulder and includes spare rib.

These recommended cuts of meat tend to be quite fatty—this is in part what makes them good for this type of cooking. However, the fat will be rendered during cooking and will begin to settle on the surface. It is worth taking the time to remove any excess fat using a large metal spoon or by floating some paper towel on the surface.

Basic principles

If possible, buy a large piece of your chosen cut and trim it yourself. Superstore packets of stewing or braising meat are often sliced too thinly to provide good-size chunks. Don't trim off too much, though, remembering that connective tissue and fat will provide richness to your stew.

Most stews and casseroles will benefit from an initial browning of the meat. This helps to impart richness to the flavor. It is best to brown the meat in batches over a very high heat. If you overcrowd the pan, the temperature will be lowered and the juices that come from the meat will actually stop the browning process. Remove browned pieces to a plate and remember to return any juices that collect on the plate back to the pan.

The next step is to add the liquid, which can vary from plain water, to stock, wine, beer, cider, or even tomatoes, among others. Some recipes will call for the liquid to be thickened, which can be done in various ways. The first is to add some flour to the pan after the meat has been browned. This will then soak up the fat and juices and will thicken the liquid when it is gradually stirred in. This is the same principle as thickening a white sauce. Alternatively, the meat can be tossed in seasoned flour before browning, which will work in the same way. Sometimes the liquid is strained off in another pan after cooking and then simmered further until reduced and thickened to taste.

A quick-fix method for thickening a stew is to make a butter and flour paste, called a beurre-manié. Mix together 1 tablespoon of softened butter with 1 tablespoon of all-purpose or plain flour until smooth. Gradually whisk this into the sauce a little at a time, until the sauce has thickened to taste.

Getting the temperature right

Stews and casseroles require very slow cooking, therefore the temperature is critical. If it's too high, the liquid will boil away before the meat is cooked. For stewing, bring the dish to a bare simmer—wait until you just see a couple of bubbles breaking the surface then turn the heat as low as possible so that the bubbling is kept to a minimum. For casseroles and oven-braised dishes, bring them to the boil on top of the stove, then transfer to the lower third of the oven at a temperature of about 275° F/Gas 1/140° C. At this temperature, an average casserole or stew will take about 2 hours to cook.

Reheating

If you have leftovers, or if you have time to make your dish ahead, cool the dish as quickly as possible, then cover and refrigerate. Bear in mind that reheating must be done only once and must be thorough. Reheat either on top of the stove over a low heat, bringing the dish to a simmer and keeping it there for at least 20 minutes, or in a preheated oven at 325° F/Gas 3/170° C for about 45 minutes. It is important to reheat thoroughly in order that any harmful bacteria that may be present are completely destroyed.

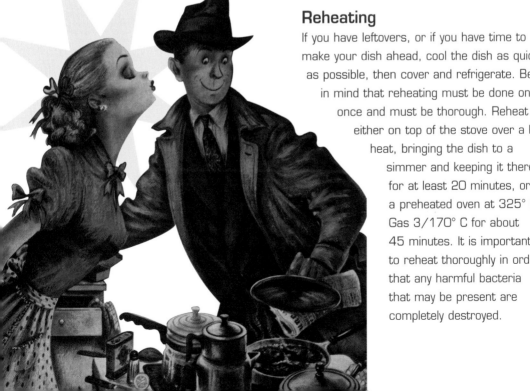

Braised Lamb Shanks

SERVES 4

4 lamb shanks	6 tablespoons olive oil
1 red onion, finely chopped	3/4 cup/6fl oz/175ml white wine
2 garlic cloves, finely chopped	1 1/2 tablespoons/1 1/2 oz/40g
small bunch of fresh thyme	chilled butter, diced
2 tablespoons fresh parsley, chopped	chopped fresh parsley, to garnish
1 teaspoon fresh rosemary, chopped	salt and freshly ground black pepper
1 tablespoon red wine vinegar	

❶ With the point of a sharp knife, gently prick the meat shanks all over. Put them into a large bowl. Mix together the onion, garlic, thyme, parsley, rosemary, wine vinegar, and 4 tablespoons of the oil. Pour this mixture over the lamb shanks. Cover and let marinate in the refrigerator overnight.

❷ Preheat the oven to 325° F/Gas 3/ 170° C. Brush the marinade off the lamb and set aside. Heat the remaining oil in a large flameproof casserole and brown the lamb shanks on all sides. Pour in the reserved marinade along with the white wine. Bring to the boil. Cover the casserole with aluminum foil then with a tight-fitting lid. Transfer to the lower third of the oven to cook for 2 hours until the meat is very tender.

❸ Lift out the lamb shanks and keep warm. Strain the liquid into a fresh pan, discarding the onion and herbs. Bring to the boil and cook for 1–2 minutes to reduce slightly. Remove from the heat and whisk in the butter, 1 or 2 cubes at a time. Taste and adjust the seasoning.

❹ Serve the lamb shanks with a little of the sauce and sprinkle with chopped parsley, to garnish.

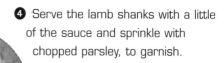

Beef Pot Roast

SERVES 4–8

2 tablespoons vegetable oil
2lb 2oz/1kg rolled brisket
(see page 34)
2 cups/9oz/250g small onions
or pickling onions
3 medium carrots, cut in half crosswise
4 celery stalks, each cut into quarters
½ large swede, cut into chunks

1¼ cups/5oz/150g medium-size
    flat mushrooms
1¼ cups/10fl oz/300ml hot stock
1 bay leaf
1 bushy sprig fresh thyme
1 tablespoon flour and 1 tablespoon
    softened butter, mixed together
    until smooth
salt and freshly ground black pepper

Preheat the oven to 275° F/Gas 1/140° C.

1 Heat the oil in a heavy-based flameproof casserole over a high heat. Add the brisket and brown well on all sides. Remove to a plate and set aside.

2 Add the onions, carrots, celery, and swede and cook for about 5–7 minutes until browned. Remove from the pan to the plate with the meat on it. Drain the fat from the pan and discard. Return the meat and vegetables to the casserole along with the mushrooms, stock, bay leaf, and thyme. Bring to the boil, cover tightly and transfer to the lower third of the oven. Cook for 3 hours.

3 Remove from the oven. Transfer the meat and vegetables to a serving platter. Put the casserole over a low heat on the stove

and gradually whisk in enough of the flour and butter mixture to thicken the sauce (you may not need all of it).

4 Cut the meat into thick slices and serve with the vegetables and sauce.

Pork Stroganoff

2 tablespoons/1oz/25g butter
1 large onion, finely sliced
14oz/400g pork tenderloin, thinly sliced
2 teaspoons fresh thyme leaves
1 garlic clove, finely chopped
2 cups/4oz/115g chestnut or button mushrooms, halved

³/₄ cup/6fl oz/175ml white wine
³/₄ cup/6fl oz/175ml sour cream or crème fraîche
2 tablespoons fresh chives or dill, chopped
salt and freshly ground black pepper

❶ Melt the butter in a medium saucepan and add the onion. Cook for 5–7 minutes over a medium heat until just starting to brown. Increase the heat and add the pork. Cook for a further 8–10 minutes until the pork is browned. If the pork releases a lot of liquid, continue cooking over a high heat until the liquid has boiled away and the meat begins frying again. Add the thyme, garlic, and mushrooms and cook for a further 5 minutes.

❷ Add the wine and bring to the boil. Cook for about 5 minutes or until reduced and syrupy. Now stir in the sour cream or crème fraîche and simmer for 2 minutes until slightly thickened. Remove from the heat and season to taste. Sprinkle over the chopped chives or dill and check the seasoning. Serve immediately with buttered noodles or rice.

Frying, broiling, grilling, and barbecuing

Certain cuts of meat are more suited to quick cooking, such as frying, broiling, grilling, and barbecuing, where meat is cooked quickly over a high heat. It is important that the meat is of good quality to produce a tender result.

The best cuts of meat for this type of cooking are steaks and chops. Again, the names and types of cuts available will vary by region, but both boneless and bone-in varieties are available. Choose a steak or chop that has a good layer of fat around the edge, but very little visible in the meat and no visible gristle.

Generally speaking, beef and lamb chops and steaks are best cooked until still pink in the center, since overcooking makes them tough and dry. This is because they have very little fat to keep them moist. Pork chops, however, should be just cooked through. It used to be considered unsafe to eat undercooked pork, but although there is a very minimal risk nowadays, pork simply tastes better and has a better texture when it is cooked through.

Steak au Poivre

SERVES 4

2 tablespoons coarsely cracked black peppercorns
4 sirloin steaks, each about 6–8oz/175–225g
2 tablespoons vegetable oil

1 shallot, finely chopped
$^{1}/_{4}$ cup/2fl oz/50ml brandy
$^{2}/_{3}$ cup/$^{1}/_{4}$ pint/150ml double cream
salt and freshly ground black pepper

❶ Put the peppercorns onto a large plate. Take each steak in turn and press one side into the peppercorns to coat. Set aside.

❷ Heat the oil in a large frying pan over a medium heat. Add the steaks, peppercorn-side-down, and cook for 3–4 minutes, then turn and cook for a further 3–4 minutes. (Cook for the shorter time for rare and the longer time for medium. Add another minute or two for well done.) Remove from the pan and keep warm, while you prepare the sauce.

❸ Reduce the heat to medium-low and add the shallot to the pan. Cook for 3–4 minutes until softened. Add the brandy and bring to the boil for 3–4 minutes until reduced and syrupy. Add the cream and bring to the boil for 1 minute until slightly thickened. Season to taste. Serve spooned over the steaks.

Steak with red wine and shallots

Omit the black peppercorns, but cook the steak as directed in the recipe for Steak au Poivre on page 41. Remove from the pan and keep warm. Add 3 finely chopped shallots to the pan and cook for 4–5 minutes over a medium heat until softened and starting to brown. Stir in 1 tablespoon of fresh thyme leaves and add 1¼ cups/10fl oz/300ml of red wine. Bring to the boil and simmer for 6–8 minutes until reduced by half. Remove from the heat and whisk in 2 tablespoons/1oz/25g of cold butter until smooth and glossy. Season to taste and serve with the steaks.

Flavored butters for grilled and fried meats

Flavored butters are a simple way to add interest to meat. Add the following ingredients to 1 rounded cup/9oz/250g of softened butter, then transfer the mixture to a sheet of greaseproof or waxed paper. Form the butter into a log shape and wrap in the paper. Refrigerate or freeze until needed. Cut into slices and top each steak or chop with 1 or 2 slices of the butter and let melt.

...for steak

Add 2 tablespoons of finely chopped mixed herbs, including parsley, chives, basil, thyme, rosemary (or any of the above on their own), and 2 crushed garlic cloves.

...for pork chops

Add 2 tablespoons of finely chopped fresh sage, 1 tablespoon of grainy mustard and 1 crushed garlic clove.

...for lamb

Roast 2 large, hot, red chilies under a hot broiler (grill) or on the barbecue until charred and tender. Let cool, then peel and deseed. In a small frying pan, dry-fry 1 teaspoon of cumin seeds until lightly toasted and fragrant. Let cool before adding to the butter along with the finely chopped chili, 1 crushed garlic clove and 1 tablespoon of chopped fresh cilantro (coriander).

Marinated Pork Chops and Mango Salsa

FOR THE MARINADE

1 scant cup/7fl oz/200ml coconut cream

2 tablespoons Thai fish sauce (nam pla)

finely grated zest and juice of 1 lime

1 stalk of lemongrass, finely chopped

1in/2.5cm piece fresh ginger, finely grated

2 garlic cloves, crushed

2 red chilies, deseeded and finely chopped

4 boneless pork loin steaks, ³/₄ in/2cm thick

FOR THE MANGO SALSA

1 large mango

1 small red onion, very finely chopped

1 red chili, deseeded and finely chopped

juice of 1 lime

2 tablespoons fresh mint, chopped

2 tablespoons fresh cilantro (coriander), chopped

1³/₄ cups/12oz/350g Thai jasmine rice

salt and freshly ground black pepper

❶ To make the marinade, mix together the coconut cream, fish sauce, lime zest and juice, lemongrass, ginger, garlic, and red chili. Put the pork steaks into a shallow non-reactive dish and pour the marinade over. Turn the steaks in the marinade to coat. Let marinate for about 2 hours—longer, if you have the time.

❷ To make the mango salsa, peel the mango. Mangoes have a large, flat stone in the middle. The flesh forms two 'cheeks' on either side of the stone. Hold the mango so that one 'cheek' of flesh is in your hand on one side and slice off the cheek on the other side—be careful as peeled mangoes are slippery. Turn the mango and repeat. Finely dice the flesh and put into a non-reactive bowl. Add the onion, chili, and lime juice. Season lightly and toss together to mix. Set aside until needed.

❸ Meanwhile, wash the rice in several changes of water until it remains relatively clear. Drain well. Put the rice into a pan with 2 cups/³/₄ pint/450ml of cold water and 1 teaspoon of salt. Cover and bring to the boil. As soon as the water boils, reduce the heat as low as possible and cook for 10 minutes. Remove from the heat and leave for a further 10 minutes. Do not lift the lid until the full 20 minutes are up. Fluff up with a fork before serving with the pork chops.

❹ Heat a ridged grill pan over a medium heat until smoking. Add the pork steaks and cook for about 4 minutes on each side until tender. Remove to serving plates.

❺ Add the mint and cilantro (coriander) to the salsa and mix well. Serve with the pork steaks and rice.

Meatloaf

SERVES 6–8

1 cup/8fl oz/250ml passata or tomato sauce
1 tablespoon tomato purée
¹/₂ cup/3oz/75g brown sugar
¹/₄ cup/2fl oz/50ml white wine vinegar
1 teaspoon Dijon mustard

1 egg
1 onion, finely chopped
¹/₂ cup/1¹/₂ oz/40g crushed water biscuits or saltines, or oatmeal
2lb 4oz/1kg beef mince
salt and freshly ground black pepper

Preheat the oven to 400° F/Gas 6/200° C.

❶ Mix the passata or tomato sauce and tomato purée with the sugar, vinegar, and mustard until dissolved.

❷ In a large bowl, lightly beat the egg, then add the onion, crushed biscuits, minced beef, salt and pepper, and ¹/₂ cup/4fl oz/125ml of the passata mixture and combine thoroughly. Shape the meat mixture into an oval and transfer to a lightly greased 2lb/900g deep loaf tin. Pour over the rest of the passata.

❸ Transfer the meat loaf to the oven and bake for 45 minutes, basting occasionally. Let stand for 5–10 minutes, turn out and serve cut into slices.

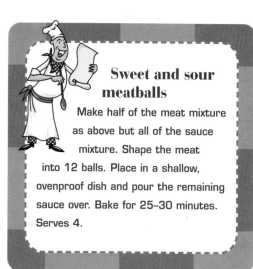

Sweet and sour meatballs

Make half of the meat mixture as above but all of the sauce mixture. Shape the meat into 12 balls. Place in a shallow, ovenproof dish and pour the remaining sauce over. Bake for 25–30 minutes. Serves 4.

How do I test my meat loaf mixture for seasoning?

Heat a little oil in a small frying pan. Add about 1 teaspoon of the mixture and cook for 3–4 minutes until cooked through. Taste and adjust seasoning accordingly.

Fish and Seafood

While we are being advised to eat less meat, we are also being urged to eat more fish to maintain good health. Fish respond well to a wide variety of cooking methods, including baking, frying, broiling, grilling, barbecuing, poaching, and roasting. Follow the recipe carefully to prepare the fish correctly for each method.

Fish, shellfish, and crustacea can be divided into the following categories:

Flat fish, which includes lemon sole, Dover sole, and flounder.

Oily fish, which includes salmon, mackerel, sardines, and herring.

Round fish, such as cod and haddock.

Large fish, including angler fish (monkfish), tuna, and swordfish.

Shellfish and crustacea, which includes clams, mussels, oysters, squid, lobster, prawns, and crab.

Many popular types of fish are becoming endangered. There is a great deal of information available from a variety of sources to help you choose fish wisely (see sources at the end of the book).

Choosing fish and where to buy

Many supermarkets have fish counters, but unfortunately some do not have a sufficient turnover to ensure the freshest produce. Dedicated fish stores are still the best source of good quality seafood.

Fresh fish should be firm and not be slimy. It should smell of the sea and not have a 'fishy' aroma. The gills should be pink and the eyes bright and clear.

Your fish stores or superstores will almost certainly be happy to prepare your chosen fish for you. They will also usually supply fish bones and trimmings for stock either free of charge or for very little cost. The addition of a few vegetables makes a very economical stock.

Storing fish

If you do not intend to cook the fish on the day of purchase, it should either be frozen or kept packed in ice in the lowest part of the refrigerator—but not for more than a day. Oily fish will deteriorate more quickly than white fish. Do not freeze for more than one month.

Cooking times for lobster

Lobsters are usually sold cooked, although they can also be bought live to be cooked at home. Lobsters have a different kind of nervous system to crabs and so are more difficult to kill humanely. They can be dropped straight into plenty of vigorously boiling salted water and cooked according to the timings shown in the chart (timing begins once the water returns to the boil after the lobster has been added).

up to 1lb 12oz/750g	15 minutes
up to 2lb 4oz/1.25kg	20 minutes
any larger lobster	an extra 5 minutes per 1lb 2oz/500g

Classic sauces for fish

Very simply cooked fish, either poached, broiled, grilled, or fried, can be enlivened with the addition of a simple sauce, for example, the Lemon Butter Sauce that accompanies the Salmon Fishcakes (see page 60), or any of those listed here.

Quick hollandaise sauce

Melt 1 cup/8oz/225g of unsalted butter in a small saucepan until simmering. Meanwhile, put 2 egg yolks, the juice of 1 lemon, and seasoning into the bowl of a small food processor or blender. Blend until well mixed and foaming—about 20–30 seconds. With the motor running, slowly pour in the hot butter until you have a thick sauce. If necessary, thin the sauce with a little hot water. Taste for seasoning—you may need more lemon juice, salt or freshly ground black pepper. Serve immediately.

Mayonnaise

Put 1 egg yolk, 1 teaspoon of wholegrain mustard, 1 tablespoon of lemon juice and seasoning into a food processor. Blend for 30 seconds until frothy. Begin adding 1 cup/8fl oz/250ml of light olive oil, drop by drop, until the mixture starts to thicken. Continue adding the oil in a slow, steady stream until all the oil has been incorporated. Taste for seasoning, adding a little more lemon juice if necessary. Thin with a little hot water if the mayonnaise is too thick. Refrigerate until needed.

Tartare sauce

Mix together 1 quantity of mayonnaise (see above), 1 teaspoon of Dijon mustard, 1 teaspoon of finely chopped green olives, 1 teaspoon of finely chopped gherkins or cornichons, 1 teaspoon of finely chopped capers, 1 teaspoon of chopped fresh parsley, 1 teaspoon of chopped fresh chives or tarragon, and some salt and freshly ground black pepper until well blended. This sauce is particularly good with deep-fried and crispy breaded fish.

Grilled Tuna with Warm Bean Salad

SERVES 4

1 cup/8oz/225g dried navy (haricot) beans
5 tablespoons extra virgin olive oil,
plus extra for brushing
1 tablespoon lemon juice
1 garlic clove, finely chopped

1 small red onion, very finely sliced
1 tablespoon fresh parsley, chopped
4 tuna steaks, about 6oz/175g each
salt and freshly ground black pepper
parsley sprigs, to garnish
lemon wedges, to serve

❶ Cover the navy (haricot) beans in at least twice their volume of cold water and soak for 8 hours or overnight.

❷ When you're ready to cook, drain and rinse the beans and place in a saucepan with twice their volume of fresh water. Bring slowly to the boil, skimming off any scum that rises to the surface. Boil the beans hard for 10 minutes, then reduce the heat and simmer for a further 1¼–1½ hours until tender.

❸ Meanwhile, mix together the oil, lemon juice, garlic, and seasoning. Drain the beans thoroughly and mix together with the olive oil mixture, onion, and parsley. Taste for seasoning and set aside.

❹ Wash and dry the tuna steaks. Brush lightly with oil and season. Cook on a preheated ridged grill pan for 2 minutes on each side until just pink in the center. Divide the bean salad between four serving plates. Top each with a tuna steak. Garnish each one with parsley sprigs and serve immediately with lemon wedges.

Oh no! My mayonnaise has started to curdle!

If your mayonnaise starts to curdle or 'split', stop adding oil. The first thing to try is to add 1–2 teaspoons of boiling water, whisk again and check. This usually re-emulsifies the mixture so that you can carry on adding oil. If this doesn't work, in a separate bowl, whisk another egg yolk and begin adding the curdled mixture, gradually, until all the mixture is added, then begin adding the oil again.

Fish and Chips

FOR THE BATTER
½ oz/15g fresh yeast
1¼ cups/10 fl oz/300ml beer
2 cups/8oz/225g all-purpose or plain flour
2 teaspoons salt

2lb/900g old potatoes
vegetable oil, for deep-frying
4 thick pieces cod fillet, about 6oz/175g
    each, preferably from the head end
salt and freshly ground black pepper
lemon wedges, to serve
parsley sprigs, to garnish

❶ For the batter, cream the yeast with a little of the beer to a smooth paste. Gradually stir in the rest of the beer. Sift the flour and salt into a bowl, make a well in the center and add the yeast mixture. Gradually whisk to a smooth batter. Cover and leave at room temperature for 1 hour until foamy and thick.

❷ For the chips, cut the potatoes into chips about ½in/1cm thick. Heat a large saucepan half filled with vegetable oil to 275° F/140° C or until a cube of bread browns in 1 minute.

Cook the chips in two batches for about 5 minutes, until they are cooked through but not browned. Drain on paper towel and set aside.

❸ Increase the heat to 325° F/170° C, or until a cube of bread browns in 45 seconds. Season the fish generously and then dip into the batter. Fry two pieces at a time for 7–8 minutes until deep golden brown

What do I do with the oil?

Let the oil cool completely, then strain and store in a clean bottle or container. The oil can be re-used to make fish and chips twice more or just for making chips, as long as you cool and strain it each time. To dispose of the oil, let it cool completely, then transfer to an empty bottle that has a tight-fitting lid (perhaps the bottle the oil came from) and throw this away.

and the fish is cooked through. Lift out, drain on paper towel and keep warm while you cook the remaining fish pieces. Keep the fish warm while you finish the chips.

❹ Increase the heat to 375° F/190° C or until a cube of bread browns in 30 seconds. Fry the chips again, in two batches, for 2–3 minutes until crisp and golden. Drain on paper towel and sprinkle with salt.

❺ Garnish the fish and chips with parsley sprigs, and serve with lemon wedges and mayonnaise (see page 48).

Thai Green Curry with Shrimps (prawns) and Coconut Rice

SERVES 4

FOR THE GREEN CURRY PASTE

5 fresh green chilies, deseeded and chopped
2 teaspoons fresh lemongrass, chopped
1 large shallot, chopped
2 garlic cloves, chopped
1 teaspoon freshly grated ginger or galangal, if available
2 cilantro (coriander) roots, chopped
$1/2$ teaspoon ground cilantro (coriander)
$1/4$ teaspoon ground cumin
1 kaffir lime leaf, finely chopped
1 teaspoon shrimp paste *(optional)*
$1/2$ teaspoon salt

FOR THE COCONUT RICE

$1^{1}/_{2}$ cups/12oz/350g Thai jasmine rice
$1^{2}/_{3}$ cups/14fl oz/400ml coconut milk
$1/2$ cup/4fl oz/120ml water
1 teaspoon salt

2 tablespoons vegetable oil
1 garlic clove, chopped
1 small eggplant (aubergine), diced
$1/2$ cup/4fl oz/120ml coconut cream
2 tablespoons Thai fish sauce
1 teaspoon sugar
1lb 2oz/500g raw shelled tiger shimps (prawns)
$1/2$ cup/4fl oz/120ml fish stock
2 kaffir lime leaves, finely shredded
about 15 Thai basil leaves, or ordinary basil

❶ To make the green curry paste, put all the ingredients into a blender or spice grinder and blend to a fairly smooth paste, adding a little water if necessary. Alternatively, pound the ingredients using a mortar and pestle until fairly smooth. Set aside.

❷ To make the coconut rice, rinse the rice in several changes of cold water until it stays relatively clear. Drain well. Put the rice into a saucepan with the coconut milk and water. Add the salt and stir well. Cover and bring to

the boil. As soon as the liquid comes up to the boil, reduce the heat as low as possible and cook for 10 minutes. Remove from the heat and leave for a further 10 minutes. Do not lift the lid until the entire 20 minutes have elapsed. Fluff up with a fork before serving.

❸ To make the thai shrimp (prawn) curry, heat the oil in a frying pan or wok until almost smoking and add the garlic. Fry until golden. Add the green curry paste that you have made and stir-fry a few seconds before adding

The clever cook's guide to peeling shrimps

To peel shrimps (prawns), first pull off the head. Hold the shrimp by its tail. With your other hand, split the shell between the legs and peel it off like a jacket. Grasp the tail firmly and carefully pull the shrimp meat from it.

the eggplant (aubergine). Stir-fry for about 4–5 minutes until softened.

4 Add the coconut cream. Bring to the boil and stir until the cream thickens and curdles slightly. Add the fish sauce and sugar and stir well until combined.

5 Add the shrimps (prawns) and stock. Simmer for 3–4 minutes, stirring occasionally, until the shrimps are just tender. Add the lime leaves and basil leaves and cook 1 more minute.

Green curry paste can be used as the basis for all sorts of Thai dishes. It is also delicious with chicken and beef. It will keep for a couple of weeks, covered, in the refrigerator if you want to make it ahead.

Sea Bass with Orange and Black Bean Sauce

SERVES 6-8

3lb/1.5kg sea bass fillets, skinned
3 oranges
2 tablespoons Thai fish sauce
5 tablespoons black bean sauce
2 garlic cloves, crushed

2 tablespoons light soy sauce
1 teaspoon grated fresh ginger
2 tablespoons sunflower oil
fresh chives, to garnish

Preheat the oven to 350° F/Gas 4/180° C.

❶ Arrange the pieces of fish in a single layer in a large baking dish.

❷ Peel two of the oranges, then chop the flesh, discarding any seeds, and put it into a bowl. Stir in the fish sauce, black bean sauce, garlic, light soy sauce, ginger, and oil.

❸ Pour the mixture over the fish, cover with aluminum foil and bake for 15–20 minutes or until the fish is cooked, and flakes easily when tested with a sharp knife.

❹ Meanwhile, slice the third orange thinly. Put the slices together in pairs. Make a cut from the rim to the center of each pair. With the cut facing you, lie one side up, at the same time turning the other side down, to make a double twist. Make more double twists in the same way until all the orange is used.

❺ Transfer the fillets of fish to a heated platter and garnish with the orange double twists and whole chives. Strain the cooking liquid into a pitcher. Spoon a little over the fish and serve the rest separately.

Spaghettini with Crab

SERVES 4

1 dressed crab, about 1lb 2oz/500g including the shell

12oz/350g dried spaghettini

6 tablespoons best quality extra virgin olive oil

1 hot red chili, deseeded and finely chopped

2 garlic cloves, finely chopped

3 tablespoons fresh parsley, chopped

2 tablespoons lemon juice

1 teaspoon lemon zest, finely grated

salt and freshly ground black pepper

lemon wedges, to serve

1 Scoop the meat from the crab shell into a bowl and set aside.

2 Bring a large saucepan of salted water to the boil and add the spaghettini. Cook according to the packet instructions until *al dente*. Drain well and return to the pan.

3 Meanwhile, heat 2 tablespoons of the olive oil in a frying pan. When hot, add the chili and garlic. Cook for 30 seconds before adding

the crab meat, parsley, lemon juice and zest. Stir-fry for a further minute until the crab is just heated through.

4 Add the crab mixture to the pasta along with the remaining olive oil and season to taste. Toss everything together thoroughly and serve immediately, garnished with the lemon wedges.

Cleaning the crab yourself

If you want to clean the crab yourself rather than buying a dressed crab, you will need a fairly large whole crab for this dish—about 1lb 12oz–2lb/750g–900g in weight. You must first snip off the eyes and mouth with a pair of scissors. Pull back each side of the top shell and pull out and discard the inedible gills. Turn the crab over and pull off the little flap called the "apron". Plunge into boiling water for 30 seconds, then twist off the apron. Pull off the top shell and clean out the stringy gills found under both sides of the shell. Lift out the crabmeat, discarding any bits of shell or cartilage. Crack the claws with a mallet or rolling pin and pull out the meat.

New England Clam Chowder

SERVES 4

1.5kg fresh clams
2 tablespoons/1oz/25g butter
1 onion, finely chopped
3 rashers bacon, finely chopped
2 medium-size potatoes, peeled and diced

4 sprigs fresh thyme
1 bay leaf
2½ cups/1 pint/600ml milk
salt and freshly ground black pepper

❶ Wash and scrub the clams. Discard any that refuse to open after a sharp tap. Pour enough water to come up to ½in/1cm in a large saucepan and add the clams. Cover with a tight-fitting lid and bring to the boil. Cook for 2 minutes, then drain, reserving 1¼ cups/10fl oz/300ml of the cooking liquid. Remove the clams from their shells, discarding any that are shut.

❷ Melt the butter in a large pan and fry the onion, bacon, and potatoes for 5 minutes until softened.

❸ Add the thyme sprigs, bay leaf, and milk. Pour in the reserved liquid and simmer the soup for 20–25 minutes until the potatoes are on the point of breaking up. Remove the sprigs of thyme and bay leaf. Season well and stir in the clams. Simmer for 1 minute, just to heat the soup through.

Oo la la!

Chowder supposedly derives its name from the French cooking pot—*chaudière*—that French settlers brought over to Canada. Unlike Manhattan chowder, which is tomato-based, the New England chowder is a creamy concoction of potatoes, onions, bacon, and clams.

Marinated Barbecued Fish Steaks

SERVES 4

4 cod or other firm white fish steaks
2 teaspoons dried oregano
zest and juice of 1 orange
1 red chili, finely chopped

1 garlic clove, crushed
4 tablespoons olive oil
salt and freshly ground black pepper

❶ Put the fish steaks into a non-reactive dish large enough to hold them in a single layer. Mix together the oregano, orange zest and juice, chili, garlic, and oil. Season with black pepper. Pour this mixture over the fish steaks and let marinate for about 1 hour.

❷ Meanwhile, light the barbecue and wait for the coals to become

hot and ready for cooking or preheat the broiler (grill) to high.

❸ Cook the steaks on the barbecue for 2–4 minutes on each side or under the broiler for 3–4 minutes until just cooked through—do not overcook.

Poached Whole Salmon

SERVES 8-10

FOR THE COURT-BOUILLON
2 carrots, sliced
2 leeks, sliced
2 medium onions, sliced
1 teaspoon black peppercorns
bouquet garni *(see page 14)*
2¼ cups/17fl oz/500ml dry white wine
2 teaspoons white wine vinegar
2¼ cups/17fl oz/500ml cold water
1 whole salmon, about 4½ lb/2kg in weight, scaled and washed

FOR THE LEMON AND WATERCRESS MAYONNAISE
3½ oz/100g watercress
1 large egg yolk
1 teaspoon Dijon mustard
finely grated zest and juice of 1 lemon
1 cup/8fl oz/250ml olive oil
salt and freshly ground black pepper

❶ To make the court-bouillon, put the carrots, leeks, onions, peppercorns, bouquet garni, wine, and wine vinegar into a large saucepan along with the water. Bring slowly to the boil and simmer gently for 20 minutes. Remove from the heat and let cool.

❷ Put the salmon into a fish kettle or large saucepan. Pour over the court-bouillon, adding more water if necessary to cover the fish. Bring slowly up to a simmer and cook for 15 minutes. Remove from the heat and leave in the liquid until cold.

❸ To make the lemon and watercress mayonnaise, bring a medium saucepan of salted water to the boil and add the watercress. Bring the water back to the boil, then drain immediately. Run cold water over

the watercress until cold. Drain well, then squeeze out as much liquid as possible.

❹ Put the watercress into a food processor along with the egg yolk, mustard, lemon zest and juice, and seasoning. Blend for about 30 seconds until the watercress is finely chopped and all the ingredients are well combined. Start adding the oil, a drop at a time, allowing each drop to be incorporated before adding the next. Carry on until you've added about half the oil. Begin adding the oil in a very thin but steady stream until you've used all the oil and have a thick sauce. Taste and add more lemon juice or seasoning, as necessary. Transfer to a serving bowl.

❺ Lift the fish from the poaching liquid and onto a large chopping board. Remove the fish head and discard. Carefully remove the skin from the uppermost section of the fish. Slide a knife between the spine and bones to remove the fillet in one piece if possible. Remove the bones and replace the fillet.

❻ Carefully flip the fish and repeat, first removing the skin, then the fillet. You now have a boneless cooked salmon. Carefully transfer to a serving platter. Serve with the mayonnaise and some boiled new potatoes.

"What can I do with the leftovers?"

It's unlikely that you'll have a lot of leftover fish, but a whole salmon might provide enough to make the following recipe.

Salmon Fishcakes

SERVES 4

9oz/250g potatoes, peeled and cut into chunks
1 tablespoon olive oil
1 onion, finely chopped
1 garlic clove, finely chopped
finely grated zest of 1 lemon
1lb 2oz/500g cooked salmon, flaked roughly
1 tablespoon fresh dill, chopped
1 tablespoon fresh parsley, chopped

1 egg, beaten
4 tablespoons all-purpose or plain flour
1 cup/2oz/50g fresh breadcrumbs
vegetable oil, for frying
salt and freshly ground black pepper

FOR THE LEMON BUTTER SAUCE
juice of 1 lemon
3/4 cup/6oz/175g butter

❶ To make the fishcakes, cook the potato in boiling salted water until tender. Drain well and mash—don't worry if there are a few lumps, as long as the potato is cooked.

❷ Heat the olive oil in a small frying pan and add the onion. Cook for 5–7 minutes until the onion is softened, then add the garlic and cook for a further minute. Add the onion and garlic mixture to the mashed potato, along with the lemon zest, cooked salmon, dill and

parsley. Season well with salt and pepper and mix gently using your hands just until the mixture holds together.

❸ Divide the mixture into eight equal portions and shape each into a cake. Beat the egg in a shallow bowl. Put the flour onto a plate and the breadcrumbs onto another plate. Dip each fishcake first in flour, then in egg, then in breadcrumbs to coat. Transfer to a plate and refrigerate for 30 minutes.

Allow to melt without boiling. Pour the butter into a clean bowl, leaving behind the white milky deposits which will be at the bottom of the pan. Discard the milky deposits, clean the pan and return the butter to it. Add the lemon juice and season to taste. If you have a hand blender, blending the sauce at this point will emulsify it and make it very light.

4 In a large frying pan, heat enough vegetable oil to cover the bottom of the pan generously. Remove the fishcakes from the refrigerator. Fry in batches for about 3 minutes each side until golden and crispy on both sides. Drain on paper towel.

5 To make the lemon butter sauce, put the butter into a small saucepan over a low heat.

6 Serve the fishcakes hot with the lemon butter sauce. These fishcakes are also delicious with the Watercress Mayonnaise from page 58.

Be prepared

You can prepare these fishcakes a day in advance but keep in the refrigerator until ready to use. Instead of salmon, try smoked haddock or cod—buy the uncolored variety.

Vegetables and Salads

Superstores have huge displays of beautiful vegetables all year round. This means that even in the dead of winter, we can have tomatoes, cucumbers, sweet corn, and green beans. Yet, as a general rule, vegetables taste best and are cheaper when they are in season and available from local suppliers.

Choosing and storing

Look for vegetables without any soft or brown or slimy spots. In general, vegetables should be firm and have good color. If possible, buy vegetables that are organic and have been grown locally, or those that are in season —they will have the best flavor.

Five servings of fruit and vegetables

The World Health Organization recommends the consumption of at least five servings of fruit and vegetables per day in order to reduce the risk of certain cancers and other illnesses. This sounds a daunting task, but it can be easily incorporated into your daily routine. Try some of the following ideas:

- Grab a piece of fruit on your way out the door.

- Keep fruit near the top of the refrigerator or in a bowl on the table where it is more visible.

- Add a handful of berries to a pot of yogurt.

- Drink a large glass of juice with your lunch.

- Add lettuce and tomato to your sandwich.

- Slice a banana or add some chopped apple or a handful of dried fruit to your morning cereal.

When you get them home, don't wash vegetables until you are about to cook or eat them. The dirt helps to preserve them. Washed potatoes are a big help in the kitchen, but don't keep as well and have fewer nutrients than unwashed potatoes. Bunched carrots with their tops should also be avoided. If you do buy them, remove the tops as soon as possible, as they drain the nutrients from the carrots.

Root vegetables and tubers, such as potatoes, sweet potatoes, and onions, should be kept in a cool, dark place. You can keep them in the refrigerator, but they tend to take a lot of space. Less hardy and leafy vegetables, such as carrots, celery, bell peppers, salad leaves, and spinach, should be kept in the vegetable compartment at the bottom of the refrigerator.

Vegetable stock

Roughly chop 1 onion, 1 leek, 2 carrots, 2 celery stalks, 1 fennel bulb, 2 tomatoes, 2 garlic cloves, and 4 large flat mushrooms. Put all the vegetables as well as 2 sprigs of parsley, 2 bushy sprigs of thyme, and 5 or 6 peppercorns into a large saucepan. Add 1.6 quarts/2¹⁄₂ pints/ 1.5 liters cold water and stir. Bring slowly to the boil, then simmer for 40 minutes. Strain and add salt to taste if using as is. Otherwise, don't season but return to a clean pan and allow to reduce as necessary before salting.

Cheese Sauce

MAKES ABOUT 1½ CUPS/12FL OZ/350ML

2 tablespoons/1oz/25g butter
¼ cup/1½ oz/40g all-purpose or
plain flour
1¼ cups/10fl oz/300ml milk

¾ cup/3oz/75g Cheddar cheese, grated
3 tablespoons fresh Parmesan cheese,
grated
salt and freshly ground black pepper

1 Melt the butter over a low heat in a medium saucepan. Add the flour and stir well to mix. Cook gently for 1–2 minutes. Do not allow to color.

2 Remove the pan from the heat and add about 3 tablespoons of the milk. Stir well using a wooden spoon, making sure to get into the corners of the pan. The mixture will appear lumpy and dry but keep stirring until smooth. Add another 3 tablespoons or so of the milk and stir again. Keep adding milk gradually and

stirring until smooth. When about half the milk is added, switch to a whisk.

3 When all the milk is added, put the pan back on a medium heat. Bring slowly up to the boil, whisking constantly, until thick and bubbling. Reduce the heat to a gentle simmer and cook for 2 minutes. Remove from the heat. Add the cheese and stir until smooth. Taste and adjust the seasoning.

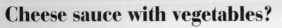

Cheese sauce with vegetables?

Cheese sauce is great with steamed vegetables, such as cauliflower or broccoli, and is also used to make macaroni cheese. Other flavors can be added, such as puréed steamed spinach or leeks and smoked ham. Including a little cream makes an even richer sauce suitable for pasta. Without the cheese, this is a classic white sauce or béchamel and can used to top a lasagna or moussaka.

Leek and Potato Soup

SERVES 4-6

2lb 4oz/1kg leeks
4 tablespoons/2oz/50g butter
1lb 2oz/500g potatoes, roughly chopped

2 cups/16fl oz/475ml vegetable stock
1¼ cups/10fl oz/300ml milk
salt and freshly ground black pepper

1 Slice the white parts of the leeks crosswise, about ¼in/5mm thick. Place in a colander and wash thoroughly, separating the rings to make sure all the grit is removed. Drain well.

2 Heat the butter in a large saucepan. Add the drained leek and stir well to coat in the butter. Cook for 10 minutes until softened. Add the potato and cook for a further 10 minutes. Add the stock, bring to the boil and reduce the heat to a simmer. Cook for 20 minutes until the vegetables are tender.

3 Add the milk, bring to the boil again and simmer gently for a further 30 minutes. Using a fork, break up some of the potato and leek to thicken the soup. Season well and serve.

What if I want a smooth soup?

If you prefer a smooth soup, put the mixture in batches into a liquidizer and blend until smooth. Reheat before serving or refrigerate and serve cold.

Vegetable Stir-fry

SERVES 4

3 cups/12oz/350g mixed prepared vegetables, such as baby corn, red bell pepper, bok choy, mushrooms, broccoli, carrot *(see below)*
2 tablespoons light soy sauce
1 tablespoon rice wine or dry sherry
2 tablespoons vegetable stock or water
2 tablespoons groundnut oil
1½ cups/12oz/350g tofu, cubed
2 garlic cloves, finely chopped

1in/2.5cm piece ginger, finely chopped
3 green (spring) onions, finely chopped
1 red chili, deseeded and finely chopped
1 teaspoon cornflour
1 teaspoon sesame oil

TO GARNISH
½ cup/2oz/50g cashews, toasted
2 green (spring) onions, finely shredded
½ cup/1oz/25g bean sprouts

❶ Halve the baby corn lengthwise, deseed and thinly slice the red bell pepper, tear or shred the bok choy, slice the mushrooms, break the broccoli into florets and slice the carrot into batons. Measure and mix together the soy sauce, rice wine, and stock, and set aside with the vegetables and other ingredients so everything is close to hand.

❷ Place the wok over a high heat until it is very hot. Carefully add the groundnut oil and swirl it to lightly coat the wok. (Heating the wok first will help to prevent the food from sticking and ensures an even heat.) Leave for a few seconds until the oil is almost smoking— a fine haze will appear.

❸ Add the tofu and, using a long-handled spatula or spoon, move it around the wok continuously until it starts to brown—this will take no more than a minute or two.

❹ Add the garlic, ginger, green (spring) onions and chili. Cook for a few seconds, continuing to stir everything in the wok.

❺ Add the prepared vegetables in the following order: carrot, broccoli, bell pepper, and mushrooms. Cook for about 1 minute

Chicken and vegetable stir-fry

Omit the tofu from the Vegetable Stir-fry and instead add 1½ cups/12oz/350g of sliced chicken breast before adding the garlic, ginger, green (spring) onions and chopped chili.

before adding the following: baby corn and bok choy. Cook for another minute, still stirring and turning everything over a high heat.

❻ Add the soy sauce mixture to the wok. Mix the cornflour with 1 teaspoon of water until smooth. Add to the wok and stir well. Bring to the boil, reduce the heat and simmer for

1 minute until thickened and everything is coated in the sauce. Remove from the heat.

❼ Add the sesame oil and mix together well. Transfer the stir-fry to serving bowls and scatter over the toasted cashews, shredded green (spring) onions and bean sprouts. Serve immediately with plain or egg-fried rice or egg or rice noodles.

Black Bean Chili with Guacamole and Cornbread

SERVES 6

1¼ cups/8oz/225g dried black turtle beans or black kidney beans
3 tablespoons olive oil
2 onions, chopped
2 garlic cloves, crushed
1 or 2 hot green chilies, deseeded and finely chopped, to taste
2 tablespoons mild chili powder
1 teaspoon ground cumin
1 teaspoon paprika
2 x 14oz/400g cans chopped tomatoes
1 teaspoon dried oregano
salt and freshly ground black pepper
sour cream to serve

FOR THE CORNBREAD
2 cups/8oz/225g self-rising flour
1⅓ cups/8oz/225g cornmeal

½ cup/3½ oz/100g granulated (caster) sugar
1 tablespoon baking powder
2 teaspoons salt
2 eggs, lightly beaten
1¼ cups/10fl oz/300ml milk
½ cup/3½ oz/100g butter, melted
1 tablespoon fresh thyme leaves

FOR THE GUACAMOLE SALSA
2 medium ripe avocados
1 small red onion, finely chopped
1 small red chili, deseeded and finely chopped
2 small tomatoes, peeled, deseeded and diced
juice of 1 lime
2 tablespoons fresh cilantro (coriander), chopped

1 Put the beans into a large bowl and cover with at least twice their volume of cold water. Leave to soak for 8 hours or overnight. Drain the beans and put into a large saucepan. Cover with fresh water and bring to the boil. Boil hard for 10 minutes, then reduce the heat and simmer for about 40 minutes until the beans are tender. Drain and set aside.

2 Heat the oil in a large saucepan. Fry the onions for 7–8 minutes until softened and browned. Add the garlic and chili and cook for 1 minute. Add the chili powder, cumin, and paprika and cook for about 30 seconds before adding the tomatoes and oregano. Simmer gently uncovered for 20 minutes. Add the beans, stir well, and simmer for a further 30–40 minutes until the chili has thickened.

3 To make the cornbread, lightly grease an 8in/20cm square cake pan. Preheat the oven to 400° F/Gas 6/200° C. In a large mixing bowl, mix together the flour, cornmeal, sugar, baking powder, and salt. Make a well in the center and add the eggs, milk, and butter. Mix lightly and quickly to form a soft batter. Fold in the thyme leaves and pour into the prepared pan. Scatter over a few thyme leaves and transfer to the preheated oven. Bake for 25–30 minutes until risen and golden. Let cool in the pan for about 5 minutes before serving cut into squares.

4 To make the guacamole salsa, peel and finely chop the avocados and put into a non-reactive bowl. Add the onion, chili, tomatoes, lime juice, and cilantro (coriander) and mix well. Cover and refrigerate until needed.

5 Season the chili to taste. Serve in bowls with a spoonful of the guacamole salsa, the cornbread, and sour cream on the side.

Roast Bell Peppers with Mozzarella

SERVES 4

4 medium red bell peppers
16 ripe cherry tomatoes, skinned
4 fat garlic cloves, finely chopped
8 anchovy fillets, drained and finely chopped
handful of fresh basil leaves, torn, plus extra, to garnish

8 tablespoons extra virgin olive oil
5oz/150g ball mozzarella in whey, drained and chopped into eight equal pieces
freshly ground black pepper

Preheat the oven to 400° F/Gas 6/200° C.

1 Cut each pepper in half lengthwise through the stem. Scoop out the seeds and membranes. Put the pepper halves onto a large baking sheet.

2 Put two cherry tomatoes into each pepper half. Divide the garlic, anchovies and basil between the pepper halves. Drizzle each with

1 tablespoon of oil. Season with black pepper (the anchovies and cheese will add enough salt). Transfer the baking sheet to the oven and cook for 40 minutes until softened and starting to brown at the edges. Remove the sheet from the oven and divide the cheese between the peppers. Return to the oven for a further 10 minutes, until the cheese is melted. Serve hot or warm with plenty of crusty bread.

Provençal Ratatouille

SERVES 4

2 bulbs fennel, quartered lengthwise
3 red onions, quartered
6 garlic cloves, unpeeled
6 tablespoons olive oil
3 zucchini (courgettes)
2 red bell peppers, deseeded
1 eggplant (aubergine)

FOR THE TOMATO SAUCE

14oz/400g can chopped tomatoes
²/₃ cup/5fl oz/150ml white wine
2 tablespoons tomato purée
6 sprigs fresh thyme
1 teaspoon sugar
salt and freshly ground black pepper

Preheat the oven to 400° F/Gas 6/200° C.

❶ You'll need two large roasting pans for this. Don't try to cram all the vegetables into one or they'll end up soggy and stewed instead of roasted. Blanch the fennel in boiling water for 5 minutes, then drain. Place the onions and fennel in a roasting pan with three unpeeled garlic cloves and half the oil. Season well.

❷ Chop the zucchini (courgettes) into ½in/1cm slices, and the peppers and eggplant (aubergine) into 2in/5cm chunks. Then, put them in the second roasting pan. Pour the remaining oil over the vegetables,

and add the rest of the garlic cloves. Roast the fennel, onion and garlic in the oven for 50 minutes, and the zucchini, peppers, eggplant and garlic for 40 minutes.

❸ Meanwhile, to make the tomato sauce, empty the tomatoes into a saucepan and stir in the remaining ingredients. Simmer for 20 minutes until reduced and thickened. Remove the thyme sprigs and stir the roasted vegetables into the tomato sauce.

A vegetarian meal with a difference

Classic ratatouille is a dish of roasted vegetables lightly covered in a rich sauce and served hot or cold. For a complete vegetarian meal, top it with slices of smoked mozzarella and place under the grill until golden.

Salad Leaves

Eating a bowl of salad every day is an excellent way to add not only a serving of vegetables to your diet, but also to increase your fiber intake. This can help to ensure a healthy digestive system.

A huge assortment of salad and salad leaves are available now from superstores. Bags of salad are a recent growth area and seem expensive, especially compared to individual lettuces. However, they provide more variety with less waste.

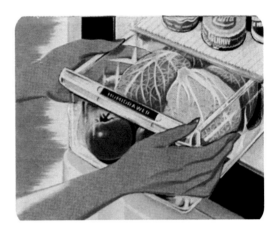

Choosing and storing

Look for leafy specimens that seem heavy for their size. They should have no brown or soft spots or evidence of insects. As with vegetables, don't wash lettuces until you need them, then drain them very well, either on paper towel or using a salad spinner, which will remove the excess water. Tear the lettuce into bite-size pieces rather than cutting it, since contact with a metal knife can cause discoloration and bruising.

Salad needs to be kept in the coldest part of the refrigerator. Wrap whole lettuces in some damp paper towel then place in a resealable plastic bag. Providing the lettuce is fresh to begin with, it will keep well in the vegetable drawer of a refrigerator for about one week.

Oil and Vinegar

Olive oil

The most popular oil by far to use in cooking is olive oil. It is believed that a diet based on olive oil, rather than on animal fat, may lead to better long-term health, and a reduced risk of heart disease and some types of cancer.

Olive oil is classified according to the level of acidity present.

Extra virgin olive oil is the finest grade and has less than 1 per cent acidity.

Virgin olive oil should have between 1 per cent and 1.5 per cent acidity.

Pure olive oil or olive oil has an acidity level above 1.5 per cent.

Many superstores offer blended oils, such as sunflower and olive oil or light olive oil. These are suitable for cooking, but their milder flavor also makes them useful for making mayonnaise, where extra virgin olive oil can sometimes be very overpowering.

Extra virgin olive oil is usually produced using a method known as cold-pressing. The olives are laid on mats and weight is applied. The resulting oil is collected and usually, although not always, filtered and then bottled. This is considered the best oil to use raw, because when heat is applied much of the delicate flavor is lost.

Vinegar

There are many types of vinegar now available, and it is useful to know the properties of each, when deciding which type to use for a particular salad dressing.

White and red wine vinegar, as you would expect, are made from wine that is cultured with a vinegar starter, or "mother", and left to mature. These are very useful multi-purpose vinegars. As with all ingredients, buy the best quality you can afford, as cheap vinegars are often highly acidic and lack flavor.

Sherry vinegar is a by-product of the sherry industry. The vinegar has a slightly nutty flavor and is a favorite among chefs.

Balsamic vinegar is made from grape must, or what is left of the grape following wine production. Balsamic vinegar has a sweet and sour flavor that is only mildly acidic. It is aged in a variety of wood barrels, and the oldest specimens are the most expensive. It thickens as it ages due to evaporation in the barrels, so a little goes a long way. It is excellent in salads, but also good used in cooking. A little reduced in a pan after cooking a steak or chop can make a great sauce on its own.

Cider vinegar is less acidic than wine vinegars, with a light apple flavor. It is good in salads, especially those containing fruit.

Rice vinegar is a very light vinegar, this time made from rice wine. It is particularly suited to oriental dishes, and for use in marinades and dipping sauces.

Malt vinegar and distilled malt vinegar are really too overpowering to use in dressings and cooking. Malt vinegar is best used as a condiment, while distilled vinegar is good for pickling, as it is neutral in flavor and so readily takes on the flavor of pickling spices.

Flavored vinegars come in a variety of flavors, from herb to fruit. It is best to buy a good quality one—the added flavors are sometimes used to disguise an unpleasant vinegar, rather than to enhance it.

Basic vinaigrette

Combine 1 teaspoon of Dijon mustard (smooth or grainy), 1 tablespoon of vinegar, juice of 1 lemon, salt and freshly ground pepper and whisk together until smooth and foamy. Whisk in 4–5 tablespoons of extra virgin olive oil a little at a time, to give a thick dressing. For a slightly thinner dressing, add the oil all at once and whisk together briefly, then again just before using. Adjust the seasoning to taste.

"Or you could even try…" Add 1 finely chopped shallot and 1 crushed garlic clove to the basic recipe above.

"And what about…" Add 2 tablespoons of finely chopped fresh herbs to the basic recipe.

Add toasted nuts for crunchy texture!

Preheat the oven to 400° F/Gas 6/200° C. Spread the nuts onto a baking sheet in a single layer. Transfer to the middle shelf of the oven and cook for 3–7 minutes (small nuts and seeds take less time than larger nuts). The nuts are done when they smell toasted and have turned a light golden color. Remove to a plate immediately to stop them cooking. Sprinkle them over salads for extra flavor.

Caesar Salad

SERVES 4

1 large egg

2 garlic cloves, crushed

2 teaspoons Dijon mustard

1 teaspoon Worcestershire sauce

4 anchovy fillets, drained and roughly chopped

juice of 1 lemon

$^1/_2$ cup/4fl oz/120ml olive oil

1 large Cos or Romaine lettuce

$^1/_2$ cup/2oz/50g fresh Parmesan cheese, grated

$1^1/_2$ cups/$3^1/_2$ oz/100g croutons (see page 77)

salt and freshly ground black pepper

1 Fill a small saucepan with water and bring to the boil. Carefully add the egg and boil for $1^1/_2$ minutes. Drain and refresh under cold running water. Let cool.

2 Put the cooled egg into a blender or the jug of a hand blender. Add the garlic, mustard, Worcestershire sauce, anchovy fillets and lemon juice along with some freshly ground black pepper. Blend until thoroughly mixed and slightly foamy. Add the oil and blend again until thickened. If the mixture is too thick (it should coat but pour off a spoon easily), add a little hot water and blend again until you get the right consistency. Taste and adjust the seasoning. Refrigerate until needed.

3 Meanwhile, wash and dry the Cos or Romaine lettuce using a salad spinner, if possible. Tear the lettuce into large pieces. Refrigerate until needed.

4 To assemble the salad, put the lettuce into a large bowl and pour over the dressing. Sprinkle with the cheese and mix together well using your hands until all the leaves are coated. Sprinkle over the croutons and mix again briefly. Serve immediately.

Don't let your salad go soggy!

If you dress this salad too early, it will wilt and become soggy. It is best assembled at the very last minute, if possible.

Fennel and Fresh Cilantro (Coriander) Salad with Orange Chili Vinaigrette

SERVES 4

2 fennel bulbs
1 large bunch fresh cilantro (coriander)
handful celery leaves
zest and juice of 1 orange
1 small red chili, deseeded and very finely chopped

1 large pinch chili flakes
1 teaspoon sherry vinegar
3 tablespoons extra virgin olive oil
1 celery stalk, very finely sliced
salt and freshly ground pepper

1 Trim a slice from the bottom of the fennel. This will release the outermost layer of the fennel, which can be discarded. Trim the tops of the fennel. Slice as thinly as possible lengthwise. Put the sliced fennel into a bowl of iced water and refrigerate for 1 hour.

2 Pick the leaves from the cilantro (coriander) and put into a bowl of iced water with the celery leaves. Refrigerate for 1 hour.

3 Meanwhile, mix together the orange zest and 2 tablespoons of the juice, the fresh chili,

chili flakes, sherry vinegar, and oil. Season well with salt and pepper and set aside.

4 Drain the fennel, cilantro (coriander), and celery leaves and put into a salad spinner (if you don't have one, drain on paper towel to remove as much water as possible).

5 Transfer the fennel, cilantro (coriander), and celery leaves to a large bowl along with the sliced celery stalk, and pour the vinaigrette over. Toss together gently to mix and serve immediately.

"Delicious with grilled fish and chicken"

Roasted Tomato and Goat Cheese Salad

SERVES 4–6

6 plum tomatoes, halved lengthwise

4 tablespoons olive oil

1 teaspoon fresh rosemary, chopped

2 tablespoons fresh basil, chopped, plus extra to garnish

1 tablespoon balsamic vinegar

1 shallot, finely chopped

3$\frac{1}{2}$ oz/100g fresh goat cheese

salt and freshly ground black pepper

Preheat the broiler (grill) to high.

❶ Arrange the tomato halves, cut-side-up, on a broiler (grill) pan or baking sheet. Mix 1 tablespoon of the oil with the rosemary. Brush this mixture over the tomatoes. Transfer to the broiler and cook for 6–8 minutes until the tomatoes are softened and starting to char round the edges. Remove from the heat and transfer the tomatoes to a large serving dish along with any juices.

❷ Mix the remaining oil with the basil, balsamic vinegar, and shallot. Pour this mixture over the tomatoes and season with some salt and freshly ground black pepper. Let cool to room temperature.

❸ Divide the tomatoes between four or six serving plates and top each one with a spoonful of goat cheese, drizzling over some of the dressing. Garnish with some fresh basil leaves and serve with plenty of bread.

Croutons

Cut 1$\frac{1}{2}$ cups/3$\frac{1}{2}$ oz/100g bread into cubes, $\frac{1}{2}$in/1cm square. Put 3 tablespoons olive oil and 1 crushed garlic clove into a large bowl. Add the bread cubes and mix together until all the cubes have a coating of oil. Transfer the bread to a large baking sheet and bake in the center of the oven preheated to 300° F/Gas 2/150° C for 20 minutes until crispy and lightly browned. Allow to cool and keep in an airtight container.

"Or you could even try..." Bacon bits; fresh herbs; cheese; or sprouted seeds.

Pasta

With so many different shapes and flavors now available, pasta (fresh or dried) makes a good basis for a nutritious meal, especially when time is pressing—and the recipe variations are endless and loved by all ages.

Types of pasta

There are literally hundreds of different shapes of pasta available at superstores and specialist delicatessens. Although virtually interchangeable, different shapes are suited to different types of sauce. For smooth sauces, choose pasta shapes that will hold the sauce, such as shells or twists. For chunkier sauces, choose smoother shapes that will mix well, such as tubes or tagliatelle.

Cooking pasta

The most important factor when cooking pasta is to use plenty of water. Fill a large cooking pot three-quarters full and add about 2 teaspoons of salt. Bring the water to a rolling boil then add the pasta—if the water is not boiling fiercely it will not return to the boil quickly enough and the pasta may stick together and will cook more slowly. You don't need to add oil to the cooking water. The salt, however, is critical—without it, the cooked pasta will be bland.

Cooking times vary enormously from one pasta shape to the next. The packet will usually offer a cooking time, but in my experience this timing is usually too long. Deduct 2–3 minutes from the suggested time and test the pasta by draining and cooling a piece under cold water. Bite into it and look at the pasta where you've bitten it—if a white line

or spot is visible, the pasta will need another minute or so. Continue boiling and test again until just cooked or *al dente*—overcooked pasta is mushy and unpleasant.

Many superstores now sell an impressive selection of fresh pasta shapes as well as stuffed pastas. These usually need to be cooked only briefly. The stuffed varieties often require only a little butter and some grated cheese to make a quick, tasty meal. Try melting some butter with 2 or 3 fresh sage leaves. Stir this butter into the cooked pasta and serve with grated fresh Parmesan and plenty of black pepper.

Make sure that the pasta is well drained—any water clinging to it will dilute your sauce. On the other hand, an oil-based sauce such as Pesto (see page 81) can seem a little dry—instead of adding more oil, reserve a couple of tablespoons of the pasta cooking water to moisten it, if necessary.

Pasta and Bean Soup

SERVES 4

3 tablespoons extra virgin olive oil, plus extra to serve
3½ oz/100g prosciutto or prosciutto di speck, roughly chopped or torn into small pieces
2 celery stalks, finely chopped
1 large potato, cubed
1 hot red chili, deseeded and finely chopped

1 fat garlic clove, finely chopped
14oz/400g can chopped tomatoes
2 x 14oz/400g cans roma (borlotti) beans
4 cups/1¾ pints/1 liter chicken stock
1½ cups/3½ oz/100g small dried pasta shapes, such as penne or farfalle
handful fresh basil leaves
salt and freshly ground black pepper

❶ Heat the oil in a large saucepan over a medium heat. Add the prosciutto and chopped celery stalks and stir well. Cook for about 5 minutes without browning.

❷ Add the potato and chili and cook for a further 10 minutes, again without browning, before adding the garlic. Cook for another minute, then add the chopped tomatoes. Set aside about one third of the beans and add the remainder to the saucepan along with the stock.

❸ Bring to the boil, then add the pasta. Cook for about 10–12 minutes until the pasta is tender. Meanwhile, in a small food processor or using a mortar and pestle, mash the remaining beans until smooth, adding a little stock from the soup, if necessary.

❹ When the pasta is cooked, add the mashed beans. Tear the basil leaves roughly and stir these in as well. Taste the soup and adjust the seasoning. Divide the soup between serving bowls and drizzle each bowl with a little extra virgin olive oil. Serve immediately with crusty bread.

Fresh Tomato Sauce

SERVES 2 WITH PASTA

2lb 4oz/1kg ripe plum or beefsteak tomatoes
3 tablespoons olive oil
1 small onion, finely chopped

1 garlic clove, crushed
2 tablespoons fresh basil, chopped
pinch of sugar
salt and freshly ground black pepper

❶ Put the tomatoes into a large bowl and pour boiling water over to cover. Leave for 30 seconds, then drain and refresh under cold water. Using a sharp knife, prick the skin of each tomato—it should split and come away easily from the tomato. If not, you may have to repeat the process for a further 30 seconds. Peel the tomatoes and chop. Set aside.

❷ Heat the oil in a large saucepan and add the onion. Cook over a medium heat for about 5 minutes, stirring often, until softened but not browned. Add the garlic and cook for a further 30 seconds. Add the tomatoes, basil, and sugar and stir well. Bring to the boil and cover. Simmer for 45 minutes. Remove the lid and simmer uncovered for 45–60 minutes until thickened. Taste and adjust seasoning.

❸ Use straight away, or let cool and refrigerate until needed. Alternatively, this sauce can be frozen for up to 3 months.

Pesto

MAKES ABOUT ½ CUP/4FL OZ/120ML

1 fat garlic clove, roughly chopped
2 tablespoons pine nuts, toasted
2½ cups/1½ oz/40g fresh basil leaves

2oz/50g piece fresh **Parmesan cheese**
½ cup/4fl oz/120ml extra virgin olive oil
salt and freshly ground black pepper

❶ Put the garlic, pine nuts, basil leaves, and Parmesan into the bowl of a food processor. Blend until finely chopped. Scrape the mixture into a small bowl, then stir in the olive oil. Season to taste and pour a thin layer of oil on top. Store in the refrigerator for one week.

Ragu Bolognese

SERVES 4-6

2 tablespoons olive oil
1 onion, finely chopped
1 carrot, finely chopped
1 celery stalk, finely chopped
1 cup/3oz/75g pancetta or smoked bacon, diced
9oz/250g lean minced pork

9oz/250g lean minced beef
1²/₃ cups/5fl oz/150ml red wine
2 tablespoons tomato purée
1¼ cups/10fl oz/300ml meat stock
3 tablespoons heavy (double) cream *(optional)*
salt and freshly ground black pepper

❶ Heat the oil in a large saucepan. Add the onion, carrot, and celery and cook over a medium heat for 10 minutes, stirring frequently, until starting to brown. Add the pancetta and continue cooking for a further 5 minutes until starting to brown. Add the minced pork and beef and cook for a further 10–12 minutes until the meat has changed color. Spoon off any excess fat.

❷ Increase the heat and add the red wine. Simmer rapidly until reduced and syrupy. Stir in the tomato purée and about half the meat stock. Bring to the boil, cover and simmer

Lasagna al forno (baked lasagne)

Make the ragu sauce as directed, omitting the cream. Ladle a little of the sauce into the bottom of a lasagna dish—just enough to lightly coat the bottom. Top with a layer of fresh or no-cook lasagna sheets. Top this with half the remaining sauce, then a second layer of pasta, the remaining sauce and the final layer of pasta (you will need about 7oz/200g of pasta). Make 1 quantity of Cheese Sauce (see page 64), omitting the cheese. Pour this over the top of the final layer of pasta. Bake in an oven preheated to 375° F/Gas 5/190° C for 35–40 minutes until golden and bubbling. Cool for 10 minutes or so before serving with a crisp green salad. Serves 4.

gently for 1½ hours, adding more meat stock as necessary to keep the mixture moist.

❸ Stir in the cream, if using, and season well.

❹ Although this sauce can be used straight away, it improves if left overnight. Alternatively, leave out the cream and freeze for up to 2 months. Defrost completely before reheating and adding cream, if using.

Ragu Bolognese

Rice

Rice is a staple food in many people's diets throughout the world. It is extremely versatile and takes on other flavors very well. It can be successfully served alongside chicken, meat, fish, and vegetables and is therefore suited to most tastes and types of diet.

Types of rice

There is a huge variety of rice available today from all over the world—to suit every type of cuisine.

Long-grain rice is probably the most widely available and is the rice to serve with most foods, especially Chinese dishes.

Basmati rice is also a long-grain rice, but it has a fine fragrance and flavor. Serve it steamed with curries and in pilafs.

Thai fragrant or jasmine rice is similar to basmati rice and is best served with Thai-style curries and stir-fries.

Risotto rice comes in a variety of forms—arborio, carnaroli, and vialone nano being the most common. All are short-grain rices and produce a creamy result, so it's best to experiment to see which one you prefer.

Paella rice looks very similar to risotto rice, but is less starchy and so produces a finished dish that is not so creamy.

Sushi rice is a another short-grain rice, and looks very much like risotto rice but has a very sticky, starchy texture. It is usually steamed, mixed with rice vinegar and sweet rice wine, then allowed to cool before it is used to make sushi.

Wild rice is not actually rice at all, but is a grass seed. Cook it for about 30–40 minutes in plenty of salted water, drain and mix with other types of rice to give an interesting texture and a nutty flavor.

Brown rice consists of the whole rice grain with the bran and germ left intact. It takes longer to cook than white rice and contains the highest percentage of fiber, vitamins, and minerals. It has a nutty flavor and pleasant bite to it when cooked.

Short-grain pudding rice is very starchy indeed and produces a delightful creamy result when slow-cooked with milk and sugar.

Perfect fluffy rice

You can cook rice by adding it to a large pan of boiling salted water and boiling for about 7 minutes, before draining, but the result is always going to be a little bit wet. For rice that is light and fluffy and not mushy, follow this method—which also works well with long-grain, basmati and jasmine rice. Measure your rice by volume, not weight. For every ½ cup/4fl oz/120ml of rice, measure an equal amount plus 1fl oz/25ml of water. Put the rice into a large saucepan that has a tight-fitting lid. Wash the rice in several changes of water until the water stays relatively clear. Drain well and return the rice to the pan. Add the measured water along with some salt. Put the lid on the pan—if it doesn't fit tightly, line it with some aluminum foil first. Bring the water to the boil and as soon as it is boiling, reduce the heat as low as possible. Cook for 10 minutes, then remove the pan from the heat and leave for a further 10 minutes. Do not lift the pan lid until the 20 minutes have elapsed or you will lose the steam that is cooking the rice. After 20 minutes, the rice will have absorbed all the water and will be tender. Fluff up with a fork before serving as needed.

Spiced Chicken Pilaf with Dried Fruit and Nuts

SERVES 4

4 tablespoons/2oz/50g butter
6 green cardamom pods, lightly crushed
1 cinnamon stick
2 bay leaves
1 cup/8oz/225g basmati rice
1¼ cups/10fl oz/300ml good quality chicken stock
1 tablespoon vegetable oil
1 medium onion, finely chopped
⅓ cup/1oz/25g flaked almonds

⅓ cup/1oz/25g pistachios, shelled and roughly chopped
¼ cup/2oz/50g dried figs, roughly chopped
1oz/25g dried apricots, roughly chopped
6oz/175g boneless chicken breast, skinned and cut into chunks
3 tablespoons fresh cilantro (coriander), chopped
salt and freshly ground pepper

1 Melt half the butter in a saucepan or casserole with a tight-fitting lid. Add the cardamom pods and cinnamon stick and cook for about 30 seconds before adding the bay leaves and rice. Stir well to coat the rice in the butter and add the stock. Bring to the boil, cover tightly and reduce the heat to low. Cook very gently for 15 minutes. Remove from the heat and let stand for another 5 minutes.

2 Heat the remaining butter and vegetable oil in a wok or frying pan. When hot, add the onion, and nuts. Stir-fry for 3–4 minutes until the nuts are beginning to brown.

3 Reduce the heat slightly and add the figs, apricots, and chicken and continue to stir-fry for a further 7–8 minutes until the chicken is cooked through.

4 Remove from the heat and add the hot cooked rice and cilantro (coriander). Stir together well. Season to taste and serve hot.

Shrimp (Prawn) Jambalaya

SERVES 6

2 tablespoons vegetable oil

2 medium onions, roughly chopped

1 green bell pepper, deseeded and roughly chopped

2 celery stalks, roughly chopped

3 garlic cloves, finely chopped

2 teaspoons paprika

11 oz/300g skinless, boneless chicken breasts, chopped

3½ oz/100g chorizo sausage, chopped

3 large tomatoes, skinned *(see page 81)*

2 cups/1lb/450g long-grain rice

3¾ cups/1½ pints/900ml hot chicken or fish stock

1 teaspoon dried oregano

2 fresh bay leaves

12 large shrimp (prawn) tails

4 green (spring) onions, finely chopped

2 tablespoons fresh parsley, chopped

salt and freshly ground black pepper

❶ Heat the vegetable oil in a large frying pan and add the onions, pepper, celery, and garlic. Cook for 8–10 minutes until all the vegetables have softened. Add the paprika and cook for a further 30 seconds. Add the chicken and sausage and cook for 8–10 minutes until lightly browned. Chop the tomatoes and add to the pan. Cook for 2–3 minutes until collapsed.

❷ Add the rice to the pan and stir well. Pour in the hot stock, oregano, and bay leaves and stir well. Cover and simmer for 10 minutes over a very low heat.

❸ Add the shrimp (prawns) and stir well. Cover again and cook for a further 6–8 minutes until the rice is tender and the shrimp are cooked through.

❹ Stir in the green (spring) onion, parsley and season to taste. Serve immediately.

Egg fried rice

Heat a wok over a high heat until smoking. Add 1 tablespoon of vegetable oil and swirl around the pan. Add 1 cup/4oz/125g of cold cooked rice per serving and stir-fry for 1 minute. Add 2oz/50g chopped bacon and ¾ cup/4oz/115g of thawed frozen peas. Continue to cook for 5 minutes. Add 2 beaten eggs per serving and cook for another 2 minutes. Add 2 tablespoons of soy sauce per serving and remove from the heat. Stir in 2 finely chopped green (spring) onions per serving and serve immediately.

Eggs

Eggs are one of the most versatile ingredients you can have in your refrigerator. They are almost a complete meal in themselves, containing protein, essential minerals, and vitamins. A couple of eggs can easily and economically be turned into a delicious breakfast, snack, or main course in next to no time.

Storing eggs

Eggs are available in different sizes and grades, as well as being battery, free-range, or organically produced (see Poultry, pages 8–9 for more information on different farming methods). Eggs keep very well for up to 3 weeks, but be sure to dispose of eggs that are past their "use by" date. Store eggs in the refrigerator, but allow them to come to room temperature, if possible, before using them. Eggs at room temperature are less likely to curdle and egg whites at room temperature will be easier to whip.

Cooking eggs

To fry an egg, melt 2 teaspoons of butter in a small frying pan (use oil or margarine if you prefer) over a medium-low heat. Tap the egg on the side of the pan to break the shell, open it by inserting your thumbs and drop the egg carefully from the shell into the pan. It should sizzle and begin to turn white round the edges immediately—if it doesn't, increase the heat slightly. Cook for about 3–4 minutes, basting the top of the egg with the butter—tip the frying pan up so that the butter collects and you can spoon it over the egg. Remove using a fish slice or spatula.

To soft boil an egg, put into a small saucepan and cover with warm water. Place

over a high heat and bring to the boil. As soon as bubbles start to rise from the bottom of the pan, set a timer as follows: 2½ minutes for very soft (soft white and yolk); 3 minutes for cooked white, still a little soft, and soft yolk; 3½ minutes for firm white and half-cooked yolk; 4 minutes for firm cooked.

To hard boil an egg, bring a small saucepan of water to the boil, then gently lower in the egg on a tablespoon. As soon as the water returns to the boil, set a timer as follows: 8 minutes for a yolk that is still slightly soft in the center but is otherwise cooked through; 9 minutes for just cooked through; 10 minutes for very firm white and yolk. Immediately drain the eggs and run cold water over them to arrest cooking. Leave until cool enough to handle before peeling.

To poach an egg, bring a medium saucepan of water to the boil. Reduce the heat so that the water is just simmering. Using a spoon, swirl the water in the pan, then break the egg as for frying and drop into the center of the swirling water. You can also add about 2 teaspoons of wine vinegar (any sort) to the water before adding the egg. The swirling helps to keep the egg white from separating too much, while the wine vinegar acts to help bind the protein in the egg white and also prevents it from separating into the water. Cook for about 3 minutes over a low heat, then remove with a slotted spoon. Drain well before serving.

To scramble an egg, whisk with 2 tablespoons of milk in a small bowl. Heat 2 teaspoons of butter in a small frying pan until foaming. Add the whisked egg mixture. Leave for about 30 seconds until beginning to set on the bottom, then stir to scrape up the cooked egg, allowing the uncooked egg to run underneath. Continue as above until the egg is just cooked and still a little soft. It will continue to cook once you remove the pan from the heat. Serve immediately.

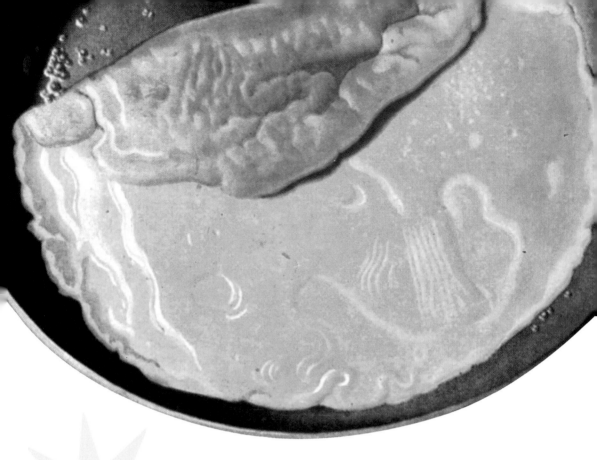

Cheese Omelette

SERVES 2

3 eggs
2 tablespoons/1oz/25g butter

½ cup/2oz/50g cheese, such as Gruyère
or Cheddar or a mixture, grated
salt and freshly ground black pepper

❶ Lightly beat the eggs with some salt and freshly ground black pepper until combined but not frothy. Heat the butter in an omelette pan or medium frying pan until melted and starting to foam. Add the egg. Stirring gently with the back of a fork, draw the egg from the sides of the pan to the center. When beginning to set, stop stirring and use the fork to gently lift the edges, allowing any uncooked egg to run underneath and set. Before the top of the omelette has completely set, sprinkle the cheese over. Remove the pan from the heat and let stand for 1 minute. Still in the pan, fold the omelette in half then slide it onto a plate—it will fold again as it falls onto the plate. Serve immediately.

Herb omelette

Finely chop about 2–3 tablespoons of fresh herbs, such as chives, parsley, chervil, and tarragon. Add to the whisked egg described in the basic recipe before cooking. Omit the cheese.

Avocado and bacon omelette

Cook the omelette as described in the basic recipe. Add a few thin slices of ripe avocado and crumble over some crisply cooked chopped bacon before folding. Omit the cheese.

Smoked ham and cheese omelette

Cook the omelette as described in the basic recipe. Add wafer-thin slices of good quality smoked ham along with the cheese before folding.

Spanish omelette

This is a different style of omelette that is slow cooked: It is sometimes called a tortilla. Peel and thinly slice or chop 2 medium potatoes and 1 large onion. Heat about 4 tablespoons of good quality olive oil in a frying pan and add the potato and onion. Cook very gently until tender, without browning if possible. Meanwhile, beat two eggs with some seasoning. Lift the potato and onion from the pan using a slotted spoon and add to the eggs. Drain all but about 1 tablespoon of the oil from the pan. Return the egg mixture to the pan, shaking it to distribute everything evenly. Cook gently until the egg is set and lightly golden on the bottom. Put a plate that is larger than the pan over the top and carefully invert the omelette on to it. Slide the omelette back into the pan, cooked-side-uppermost, and continue to cook until the bottom is set and golden. This omelette can be served hot, warm or cold with salad and crusty bread. Serves 2.

Crêpes suzette

Make the pancakes as directed (see opposite), adding the zest of 1 orange and 1 tablespoon of sugar to the basic batter mixture. Cook the pancakes and stack between sheets of paper towel. Now mix the zest of another orange and a lemon, 1 tablespoon of sugar and ½ cup/5fl oz/150ml of orange juice together. Heat a large frying pan and add 4 tablespoons/2oz/50g of unsalted butter. When melted and foaming, add the juice mixture and bring to the boil for 1–2 minutes until slightly thickened. Fold the pancakes into triangles and add to the pan to heat through. Pour over 3 tablespoons of Cointreau or other orange liqueur and set alight. Serve, once flames have subsided, with pouring cream.

Potato pancakes with creamy mushrooms

Mash and season 1lb 2oz/500g cooked floury potatoes. Whisk in 3 egg yolks, 2 tablespoons/1oz/25g of butter, ½ cup/ 2oz/50g/ of all-purpose or plain flour, and approximately 5 tablespoons of milk to give a soft mash. In a clean bowl, whisk 3 egg whites until stiff peaks form, then fold into the mash. Heat a little oil in a large frying pan and add large spoonfuls of the batter. Cook for 2 minutes each side until browned, crisp and slightly souffléd. Keep warm until ready to serve.

Heat 2 tablespoons of olive oil in a large frying pan and add 1¾ cups/7oz/200g of halved button or chestnut mushrooms. Cook over a high heat until browned and softened. Add rounded ½ cup/5fl oz/150ml of crème fraîche or sour cream and 1 tablespoon of creamed horseradish. Stir in 2 tablespoons of chopped fresh chives, season to taste and serve with the potato pancakes. Serves 4 as a main course or 6 as a starter.

Pancakes

MAKES 8 X 8IN/20CM PANCAKES

1 cup/4oz/115g all-purpose or plain flour
pinch of salt
2 medium eggs, beaten

1¼ cups/10fl oz/300ml milk
vegetable oil, for greasing

❶ Sift the flour along with the pinch of salt into a mixing bowl. Add the eggs and half the milk. Whisk until thick and smooth. Gradually whisk in the remaining milk until you have a smooth batter the consistency of thin cream. Cover and let stand for 20–30 minutes.

❷ Lightly oil an 8in/20cm crêpe pan or frying pan. Put the pan over a medium heat. Pour in about 2 tablespoons of the batter and swirl the pan to coat the bottom thinly and evenly. Cook for about 1 minute, until the edges appear dry, then carefully flip or turn the pancake, allowing it to cook on the other side for about 30 seconds.
Repeat with the remaining

batter, stacking pancakes between sheets of paper towel as you go and keeping them warm until ready to serve.

Quiche Lorraine

FOR THE PASTRY

1½ cups/6oz/175g all-purpose
or plain flour
pinch of salt
⅓ cup/3oz/75g butter, diced
2–3 tablespoons cold water, to mix

FOR THE FILLING

2 cups/6oz/175g pancetta or smoked
bacon, diced
1½ cups/5oz/150g Gruyère cheese, grated
3 egg yolks
1¼ cups/10fl oz/300ml heavy
(double) cream
2 teaspoons Dijon mustard
salt and freshly ground black pepper

1 To make the pastry, sift the flour and salt into a large bowl and add the butter. Rub together until the mixture resembles coarse breadcrumbs. Add 2 tablespoons of the water and bring the dough together, adding a little more water if it seems dry. Turn the mixture onto a lightly floured surface and knead briefly until smooth. Wrap in plastic wrap (clingfilm) and refrigerate for 30 minutes.

2 Roll out the pastry into a large circle measuring about 11–12in/28–30cm in diameter. Use the pastry to line a 9in/23cm fluted tart pan. Press the pastry into the corners and the sides of the pan and remove the excess. Prick the base all over with a fork and transfer the lined tart pan to the refrigerator for 20 minutes. Preheat the oven to 400° F/Gas 6/200° C.

3 Remove the pan from the refrigerator and carefully line with aluminum foil or greaseproof paper. Add ceramic baking beans or dried pulses or rice. Put the tart pan onto a baking sheet and transfer to the oven. Cook for 12 minutes, then remove the foil or paper and beans. Return to the oven for a further 10 minutes until the pastry is golden. Reduce the oven temperature to 350° F/Gas 4/180° C.

4 For the filling, heat a frying pan over a high heat and add the pancetta or smoked bacon. Cook for 5–7 minutes until golden. Drain on paper towel. Sprinkle the pancetta or smoked bacon evenly over the pastry case. Sprinkle the cheese evenly on top.

5 Whisk the egg yolks with the cream, Dijon mustard, and black pepper. Be careful not to add too much salt, as both the pancetta and cheese are salty. Pour this mixture evenly over the cheese and transfer the pan to the middle of the oven. Cook for 25–30 minutes until golden and just set. Serve hot or cold.

Cheese Soufflé

3 tablespoons/1¹/₂ oz/40g butter,
plus extra for greasing
4 tablespoons/1oz/25g fresh Parmesan
cheese, grated
¹/₄ cup/2oz/50g all-purpose or plain flour
1¹/₄ cups/10fl oz/300ml milk

4 eggs, separated
1 cup/3¹/₂ oz/100g Gruyère, Emmental,
or Appenzeller, grated
2 tablespoons fresh chives, chopped
salt and freshly ground black pepper

Preheat the oven to 375° F/Gas 5/190° C.

❶ Set the shelves in the oven so that the top shelf is in the center of the oven with no shelves or grill pan above it.

❷ With the extra butter, generously grease a 6¹/₄ cups/2¹/₂ pint/3 liter soufflé dish. Sprinkle the Parmesan cheese into the dish and turn it so that the cheese sticks to the butter on the sides and bottom. Set aside.

❸ Melt the remaining butter in a medium saucepan. Add the flour and stir well until smooth. Cook gently for 1–2 minutes.

❹ Remove the pan from the heat and add about 3 tablespoons of the milk. Stir well using a wooden spoon. The mixture will appear lumpy and dry but keep stirring until smooth. Add another 3 tablespoons of the milk and stir again. Keep adding milk gradually and stirring until smooth. When about half the milk is added, switch to a whisk and continue adding the milk in small amounts.

❺ When all the milk is added, return the pan to a medium heat. Bring slowly up to the boil, whisking constantly, until thickened and bubbling. Reduce the heat to a gentle simmer and cook for 2 minutes, then remove. Cover and let cool for 5–10 minutes.

❻ Add the egg yolks and whisk in thoroughly. Add the cheese and chives and stir together. Season generously—the egg white is going to dilute this mixture, so it's okay to over-season.

❼ Put the egg whites into a very clean bowl and whisk until stiff peaks form. Transfer a large spoonful of egg white to the cheese mixture and fold together. This will slacken the mixture and make it easier to fold in the egg white. Add the remaining egg white and fold together carefully, but thoroughly.

❽ Pour the mixture into the soufflé dish and transfer to the center shelf of the oven. Bake for 25–30 minutes until well risen but firm. It should be soft, not liquid, in the middle.

Meringues

MAKES ABOUT 8 PAIRS

3 egg whites
pinch of salt
³/₄ cup/6oz/175g granulated (caster) sugar

drop of vanilla extract
1 scant cup/7fl oz/200ml heavy
(double) cream

Preheat the oven to 250° F/Gas ½/120° C.

1 Line two baking sheets with non-stick baking parchment. Set aside.

2 Using an electric whisk, beat the egg whites with the salt until stiff. Check this by lifting the whisk from the mixture and holding it upside down. If the tip of the egg white falls, the peak is soft. If it stands firm, it is stiff.

3 Add about half the sugar and whisk thoroughly. Keep whisking until the egg white no longer appears grainy and is very shiny and smooth. Add more sugar, about 1 tablespoon at a time, whisking thoroughly between additions until all of it has been added. Add the vanilla extract. Keep whisking until the

mixture is smooth, thick and glossy. If the sugar is not whisked in thoroughly enough, it will melt and leach out during cooking, making a very sticky mess.

4 Place 16 large spoonfuls of the mixture onto the prepared baking sheets, leaving plenty of space in between. Use the back of the spoon to make nice peaks on the tops. Transfer to the oven and cook for 1 hour, switching the baking sheets over half-way through, then switch off the oven and leave until cold. This will give the meringues a crisp outside and chewy, "marshmallowy" inside. If you prefer them crisper, cook for 1½ hours then leave until cold.

How do you separate eggs?

If separating a large number of eggs, it is safest to use three bowls. Break the egg over one bowl and separate the white into it, and then transfer the yolk to a second bowl. Finally, move the egg white to the third bowl. Separate each egg this way over the first bowl before moving the yolk and white to their separate bowls, so that if any yolk drops into the white over the first bowl, only one egg will be lost.

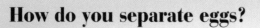

5 Whip the heavy (double) cream until soft peaks form. Take one meringue and put a large spoonful of cream on the base. Sandwich with another meringue and set aside. Repeat with all the meringues and all the cream. Serve immediately. The meringues will keep, without the added cream, in an airtight container for up to one week.

Raspberry surprise

Using about half the meringues for the basic recipe, roughly crush them and set aside. Whip 1¼ cups/10fl oz/300ml of heavy (double) cream in a large bowl until soft peaks form. Fold in the crushed meringues along with 2 cups/9oz/250g of raspberries. Serve immediately.

Italian meringue

This is a variation on the cooking method outlined in the basic recipe. Put all the ingredients into a large, heatproof bowl. Set the bowl over a saucepan of simmering water—the bowl should not touch the water. Using an electric whisk, begin whisking the mixture. Carry on until the mixture has become smooth, thick, glossy and hot—about 10–15 minutes. Remove the bowl from the heat and continue whisking for a further 5 minutes until the mixture cools down. Transfer to prepared baking sheets as above, but cook for only 30 minutes before turning the oven off. This mixture is already cooked when it goes in the oven and therefore only needs to dry out.

Pavlova with tropical fruit

Follow the recipe for meringues as above, but when all the sugar has been added, whisk in 1 teaspoon of cornstarch (cornflour) and 1 teaspoon of wine vinegar. Spread all of the mixture onto a prepared baking sheet, in an 8in/20cm diameter circle, making a depression in the center. Transfer to the oven and cook for 2 hours, then switch off the oven and leave until cold.

Whip the cream and use to fill the meringue shell. Peel and chop 1 large mango, 2 papayas, 2 kiwis and use to top the cream. Scoop the seeds from 3 passion fruits and drizzle over the top. Serve immediately.

Baking

The art of baking is feared by many, usually unnecessarily so. However, with a few key pieces of equipment, a handful of ingredients and essential basic skills, you will fill your home with the warm aroma of breads and cakes that will look and taste absolutely delicious.

Main types of flour

Most baked goods are based on flour and it is important to choose the right flour for the job. In general, there are three main types of flour, which vary according to the percentage of the wheatgrain they contain.

Whole-wheat is 100 per cent of the wheatgrain milled with nothing adding or removed.

Brown contains 85 per cent of the wheatgrain with some bran and germ removed.

White contains 75 per cent of the wheatgrain with most bran and germ removed.

Other types of flour:

Malted grain is whole-wheat or brown flour to which malted grains have been added.

Stone-ground is ground in the traditional manner between stones, rather than with stainless steel wheels.

Organic farming is at present unregulated, and the definition of what organic actually means varies from region to region. This can differ from country to country and it is advisable to check with your local authority or government as to how they regulate organic farming.

In addition, flour varies according to its protein content. Protein, when combined with water (or other liquid), forms gluten. Gluten determines a dough's elasticity and gas-retaining properties. Low-protein flours are said to be soft while high-protein flours are stronger. Softer flours are good for cakes and pastries, while strong flours are used for breads, pizza, and pasta.

Flour may also contain certain additives, including bleaching agents for whitening (so-called 'aged' flour is also white, but has been allowed to oxidize—it will be more expensive). Bleaching agents do not alter the nutritional content of the flour but can diminish its gluten strength. Maturing agents can be added to strengthen flour for breadmaking, although this is usually restricted to commercial bread. Vitamin and mineral enrichment is also common to replace those nutrients lost through the milling process.

Understanding flour labels

A number of different varieties of flour are available, depending on their ultimate use:

Cake flour is a very finely milled soft flour, which is usually bleached and enriched.

Pastry flour is also a fine-milled soft flour, best used for pastry as well as cookies, biscuits, and some cakes.

All-purpose or plain flour is milled from hard flour, or a mixture of hard and soft flour, and gives the best results for a wide variety of recipes, from some yeast breads and quick breads, to pastries, cakes, and cookies.

A useful hint on cake pans

Baking pans are available in a variety of materials, including aluminum, enamel, non-stick, and even silicone. Choose the best quality that you can afford. Beware, however, that pans, especially cake and loaf pans, vary in shape and size and that this will affect the performance of the recipe. For example, a 7in/23cm round cake pan with a depth of 1in/2.5cm may actually have a diameter of 7½in/24cm. It doesn't sound like much, but it means the pan has 15 per cent more capacity —your cake will cook more quickly and be thinner.

High gluten flour or strong flour has a high protein content.

Self-rising or phosphated flour has had salt and baking powder added and is best used where extra raising is needed, as in all-in-one cake mixes.

Many of these flours will be available in white, whole-grain or brown varieties. A number of specialty wheat flours are also available, including rye, durum, and semolina.

Storing flour

Flour should be stored in an airtight container because it is attractive to pests. It does not have an indefinite shelf life and should not be kept for longer than 6 months at room temperature. Flour can be successfully frozen, in which case it will keep for up to 2 years. Return it to room temperature before using.

Do not combine a new bag of flour with the remains of an old one that has been stored for some time, since anything present in the stored flour will pass to the new flour.

Equipment

If you do a lot of baking, the following list of equipment is essential:

- Mixing bowls of varying sizes
- Wooden spoons
- Spatula
- Electric whisk
- Flour sifter
- Baking sheet
- Swiss roll pan
- Muffin pan
- Baking pans in a range of sizes
- Piping bag and nozzles for decorating
- Non-stick baking parchment

LINING THE CAKE TIN

SANDWICH PAN	CAKE PAN

Place the pan on greasproof paper and draw round it with a pencil.

Cut just inside the pencil mark with scissors.
Cut a strip of paper long enough to go round the pan and over-lap about 1 inch.

For a sandwich pan the strip should
be about 2 inches deeper than the tin.

For a cake pan the strip should be
about 2½ inches deeper than the tin.

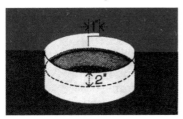

Lay the strip flat on the table and turn up ½ inch and crease. Snip diagonally to the fold.

Brush inside the pan with melted lard or vegetable cooking fat, using a pastry brush.
Insert strip so that the snipped part lies flat on the base.

Put the circle in place and lightly brush over the paper on the base and sides with fat.

White Bread

6 cups/1½ lb/675g strong white bread flour, plus extra for dusting
1 tablespoon/½ oz/15g butter
1 tablespoon salt
2 teaspoons instant (easy-blend) yeast

2 scant cups/15fl oz/425ml hand hot water
oil for greasing, and extra in an oil sprayer, if possible

❶ Generously grease either one 2lb/1kg loaf pan or two 1lb/450g loaf pans. Sift the flour into a large bowl and add the butter. Rub the butter into the flour until combined. Stir the salt and yeast into the flour and stir well until thoroughly combined.

❷ Make a well in the center of the flour mixture and pour in the water. Mix to a dough, starting off with a wooden spoon and then using your hands to bring the dough together into a slightly sticky ball.

❸ Tip the dough onto a lightly floured surface and begin kneading the dough. Push the dough away from you with the heel of your hand, then pull it back towards you using the opposite hand. Repeat for about 10 minutes until the dough becomes very smooth and elastic and is no longer sticky. Alternatively knead the dough using a mixer fitted with a dough hook for

6–8 minutes until smooth and elastic. Form the dough into a neat ball.

❹ Transfer the dough to a clean, lightly oiled bowl. Using an oil sprayer, lightly spritz the surface of the dough. Otherwise, put a little oil on your hand and rub it gently over the surface. This will help to prevent a skin from forming.

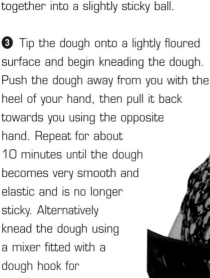

❺ Cover the bowl with a clean dish towel or some plastic wrap (cling film). Let rise for about 1 hour, or until doubled in size.

❻ Turn the dough out of the bowl onto a clean surface and knead for 3–4 minutes. Now either shape the dough as it is or divide it in two. Either way, shape the dough into an oblong then fold one end into the center and fold the other end in on top. Put into the prepared pan or pans, seam-side-down.

❼ Sprinkle the top with a dusting of flour, then set aside in an oiled polythene bag until the dough rises to the top of the pan(s). This will take 30 minutes to 1 hour, depending on the room temperature. Meanwhile, preheat the oven to 450° F/Gas 8/230° C.

❽ Transfer the loaf or loaves to the center of the oven and bake for 40–45 minutes for the large single loaf and 35–40 minutes for the two smaller loaves. The bread is cooked when it is a rich golden brown and sounds hollow when tapped on the bottom. Remove from the pan(s) and return to the oven for 5 minutes to crisp the sides and base. Let cool completely before serving.

All you need to know about yeast

Fresh yeast is available from healthfood shops and superstores with a bakery department, but must be absolutely fresh or it will be unreliable. Commercial yeast is a by-product of the brewing industry. When fresh, it should be creamy colored, moist and firm with a strong 'yeasty' smell. If it is crumbly or has discolored dark patches, it is probably stale. Fresh yeast is usually dissolved in the liquid specified in the recipe, along with a little sugar and/or flour until it is frothy and active before being added to the flour. It keeps only a few days wrapped up in the refrigerator, but will freeze for up to 3 months in an airtight container or bag.

Dried yeast is fresh yeast that has been dried into small balls. Use it in the same way as fresh yeast, by dissolving in the liquid and leaving it to froth before adding to the flour.

Instant (easy-blend) yeast is also a form of dried yeast. It is highly reliable and very easy to use, as it is added directly to the flour. It's important to abide by the use-by date on the packet but the good news is that it will keep for up to 6 months in the freezer and, because it doesn't stick together, can be used straight from frozen.

Basic Whole-wheat Loaf

MAKES 1 LARGE OR 2 SMALL LOAVES

4 cups/1lb/450g strong whole-wheat
bread flour, plus extra for dusting
2 teaspoons salt
1 teaspoon brown sugar

2 teaspoons instant (easy-blend) yeast
about 1½ cups/12fl oz/350ml
hand hot water
oil, for greasing

Preheat the oven to 400° F/Gas 6/200° C.

1 Generously grease either one 2lb/1kg loaf pan or two 1lb/500g loaf pans. Set aside. Put the flour, salt, sugar, and yeast into a large bowl and mix together well. Add the water and mix to a dough. You may not need all the water, as whole-wheat flour varies enormously in its absorption. If the dough seems dry, add a little more water.

2 Knead briefly, until just smooth, then either shape the dough as is, or divide it in two. Shape the dough into an oblong then fold one end into the center and fold the other end in on top. Put into the pan(s), seam-side-down.

3 Sprinkle the top with a dusting of flour, then set aside in an oiled polythene bag until the dough rises to the top of the pan(s). This will take 30 minutes to 1 hour, depending on the room temperature.

4 Bake the loaf or loaves for 45 minutes for the larger size and 35 minutes for the smaller loaves. Turn the loaf or loaves out of the pan(s) and return to the oven, upside-down, for about 5–10 minutes until the sides and bottom are crisp. Check the loaves are cooked by tapping the bottoms—they should sound hollow. Let cool on a wire rack.

How do I oil a plastic bag?

To oil a plastic bag, turn it inside out and rub all over with a piece of folded paper towel that has been dipped in a little vegetable oil. Turn the bag right side out again to use.

Soda Bread

MAKES 1 LOAF

2¼ cups/9oz/250g whole-wheat flour
¾ cup/3½ oz/100g all-purpose or
plain flour
1 teaspoon salt

2 teaspoons baking soda
2 tablespoons butter, plus extra for greasing
1¼ cups/10fl oz/300ml buttermilk

Preheat the oven to 400° F/Gas 6/200° C.

❶ Lightly grease a baking sheet.

❷ Sift together the flours, salt and baking soda. Rub in the butter, then stir in most of the buttermilk—you may need more or less depending on the flour. The dough will be quite lumpy at this stage.

❸ Turn the dough onto a floured surface and knead for about 3 minutes until smooth and slightly sticky. Shape into a lightly flattened ball about 8in/20cm in diameter. Transfer to the baking sheet.

❹ Using a sharp knife, cut a deep cross in the top of the loaf, without cutting all the way through. Transfer to the center of the oven.

❺ Bake for 30–35 minutes until the bread is deep golden and sounds hollow when tapped on the bottom. Cover with foil after about 20 minutes if the bread begins to overbrown.

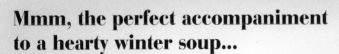

Mmm, the perfect accompaniment to a hearty winter soup...

Soda bread is especially good served with wholesome soup and is very quick to make. It is best eaten on the day it is made, but it toasts well on day two.

Pizza

MAKES 2 X 10IN/25CM PIZZAS

2 cups/8oz/225g strong white bread flour, plus extra for kneading

1 teaspoon salt

1 teaspoon instant (easy-blend) yeast

1 tablespoon olive oil, plus extra for drizzling

³/₄ cup/6fl oz/175ml warm water

❶ Mix the flour, salt, and yeast together in a large bowl. Make a well in the center and add the oil along with ¹/₂ cup/4fl oz/120ml of warm water. Mix together, using a wooden spoon at first and then using your hands. Add the remaining water, if necessary, to make a soft, slightly sticky dough.

❷ Turn the dough onto a floured work surface and knead for 7–8 minutes until smooth and elastic. Form the dough into a neat ball and transfer to a clean, lightly oiled bowl. Cover and let rise for about 1 hour or until doubled in size.

❸ Meanwhile, put the top shelf of the oven as high as it will go, allowing room for a baking sheet and the pizza. Preheat to 475° F/Gas 9/ 240° C. If you have a pizza stone, put this on the top shelf to preheat.

❹ When the dough has risen, turn it onto a clean work surface and knead briefly. The dough should be very elastic. Put a piece of non-stick

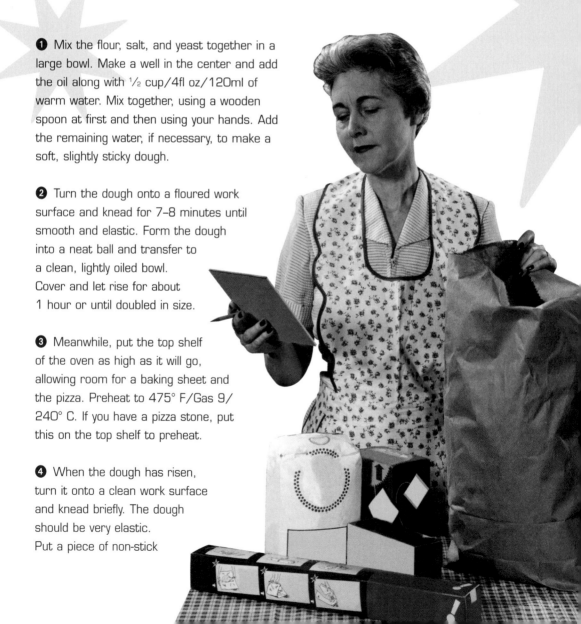

Pizza toppings

Spread each pizza base with 2 tablespoons of tomato purée,
1 cup/3½ oz/100g of lightly sautéed, sliced mushrooms,
1½ cups/3½ oz/100g of sun-dried tomatoes, 2oz/50g of sliced
pepperoni or other cured sausage and 5oz/150g of drained and
torn mozzarella cheese. Season well, drizzle with extra virgin olive oil
and bake as above.

Thinly slice 1lb/450g of mixed fresh tomatoes, such as plum, beefsteak, red,
yellow and orange cherry tomatoes. Lay on 2 or 3 layers of paper towel and
let drain. Scatter half over each pizza base, then scatter 5oz/150g of
mozzarella in brine (which has been drained and broken into small pieces)
over each pizza. Scatter each with a handful of roughly torn fresh basil
leaves and drizzle with extra virgin olive oil. Season well and bake as above.

Alternative to garlic bread

Mix together 2 tablespoons of olive oil and 1 crushed garlic clove. Brush this
mixture over each pizza base. Roughly chop a couple of sprigs of rosemary and
scatter these over each base along with 2 teaspoons of coarse sea salt or sea
salt flakes. Bake for 8–10 minutes until risen and golden.

baking parchment paper onto a large baking sheet. Divide the dough in two and put one piece in the center of the baking parchment. Using wet hands, begin to stretch and flatten the dough, turning the baking sheet often, until you have a rough circle measuring about 10in/25cm. Cover the dough with your chosen toppings (see above) and transfer the baking sheet to the oven (if you have a pizza stone, transfer the dough still on the baking parchment directly to the pizza stone). Bake for 10–12 minutes until the dough is golden and the topping is bubbling. Remove from the oven, cut into slices and serve immediately. Repeat with the second piece of dough.

❺ Alternatively, if your oven and baking sheet are large enough, make one pizza measuring approximately 15in/37.5cm and bake as directed above.

Sponge Cake

SERVES 8–10

½ cup/4oz/115g butter, softened, plus extra for greasing
½ cup/4oz/115g granulated (caster) sugar
2 medium eggs, lightly beaten
½ teaspoon vanilla extract

¾ cup/4oz/115g cake or self-rising flour
raspberry or strawberry jam or lemon curd *(see opposite)*, to serve
confectioner's (icing) sugar, to decorate

Preheat the oven to 350° F/Gas 4/180° C.

❶ Grease two 7in/18cm sandwich pans, using the extra butter. Line the base of the pans with non-stick baking parchment paper. Set aside.

❷ In a large mixing bowl, beat together the butter and sugar until light in color and fluffy. This step is very important in ensuring that the finished cake is light and airy—the air beaten in at this stage is very easily lost, so make sure you do this thoroughly. It will take about 5 minutes with an electric whisk.

What's the difference between vanilla extract and vanilla essence?

Vanilla extract is made using whole vanilla beans and seeds, while vanilla essence or vanilla flavor essence is made using a chemical substitute. Vanilla from Madagascar is the best quality. Also available are vanilla pods and vanilla powder.

❸ Begin adding the egg, about 1 teaspoon at a time. Beat in thoroughly before adding the next teaspoon. If the mixture begins to curdle, add about 1 tablespoon of the flour, then continue until all the egg is incorporated. Beat in the vanilla extract.

❹ Sift the flour into the bowl and fold in carefully but thoroughly using a wooden spoon. The mixture should drop easily off the spoon. If it doesn't, you may need to add a little hot water or milk (about 2–3 teaspoons) to loosen it slightly.

❺ Divide the mixture between the prepared cake pans and transfer to the center of the preheated oven. Bake for 30–35 minutes until risen and golden. The cake should spring back when pressed in the middle with a finger and a skewer inserted into the middle of the cake should come out clean. If any mixture clings to it, return to the oven for a further 5 minutes, then test again.

❻ Let cool in the pans for 10 minutes, then transfer to a wire rack until cold. To serve, put one cake on a serving plate and top with about 2 tablespoons of your chosen jam. Top with the second cake and sprinkle with confectioner's (icing) sugar. Serve cut into wedges.

Lemon filling

Fill the cake with this fresh lemon spread as an alternative to jam. In a heatproof bowl, mix together the finely grated zest and juice of 1 large lemon, ¾ cup/3oz/ 75g of granulated (caster) sugar, 2 large lightly beaten eggs and 4 tablespoons/ 2oz/50g of diced unsalted butter. Put the bowl over a pan of simmering water, making sure that the bottom of the bowl does not touch the water. Stir often until everything is mixed together, then continue stirring often until the mixture thickens—about 20 minutes. Let cool, then use to sandwich the sponge cakes together.

All-in-one sponge

Prepare the sandwich pans as directed for the Sponge Cake on page 108. In a large mixing bowl, put ³/₄ cup/4oz/ 115g of cake or self-rising flour, 1 teaspoon of baking powder, ¹/₂ cup/ 4oz/115g of butter, ¹/₂ cup/4oz/115g of granulated (caster) sugar, 2 large eggs, and ¹/₂ teaspoon of vanilla extract. Preheat the oven to 350° F/Gas 4/180° C. Whisk on a low speed until well blended. Increase the speed and beat for 2 minutes. The mixture should drop easily from a wooden spoon. If not, add a little hot water or milk as directed on page 109. Divide the mixture between the pans and bake in the center of the oven for 30–35 minutes or until a skewer comes out clean. Cool in the pans for 10 minutes, then turn the cakes onto a wire rack and leave until cold. Serve as above, with jam and confectioner's (icing) sugar.

Chocolate sponge Sift 2 tablespoons of quality cocoa powder along with the flour in either of the previous sponge mixes.

Coffee and walnut sponge Omit the vanilla extract and substitute with 1 tablespoon of Camp coffee or strong espresso along with ¹/₂ cup/2oz/50g of finely chopped walnuts.

What's the difference between the two cakes?

The main difference between the Sponge Cake and All-in-one Sponge is the addition of baking powder. Classic sponge mixture is made in such a way as to incorporate a lot of air, creaming the butter and sugar together, then carefully adding the egg and folding in the flour. The all-in-one sponge needs the extra boost of the baking powder to ensure a good rise.

Why should the eggs be at room temperature before I begin?

Can I use margarine?

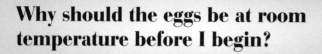

Cold eggs are much more likely to curdle than those allowed to come to room temperature before they are used.

Although both recipes call for the use of butter, soft margarine can be substituted (not low-fat versions, however, which have too much added water). The difference is that the butter-based cakes will have a richer flavor and a denser texture compared to the margarine-based cakes. Surprisingly, butter-based cakes can also be less moist.

Chocolate Buttercream Icing

MAKES ENOUGH TO FILL AND COVER A
7IN/18CM SPONGE CAKE (TWO LAYERS)

$3^{1}/_{2}$ oz/100g dark chocolate
$^{3}/_{4}$ cup/6oz/175g unsalted butter, softened
3 cups/1lb/450g confectioner's
(icing) sugar

6 tablespoons cocoa powder
2 tablespoons milk

1 Break the chocolate into even-size pieces and put into a heatproof bowl. Set the bowl over a pan of simmering water, ensuring that the bottom of the bowl doesn't touch the water. Let the chocolate melt without stirring, then remove the bowl from the heat and let cool for about 5 minutes.

2 Meanwhile, beat the butter until very soft and light-colored. Sift the confectioner's (icing) sugar with the cocoa powder and add this mixture, about one third at a time, alternating with the milk. The mixture will be very thick. Now add the cooled chocolate and mix together thoroughly—you may find a rubber spatula useful for this. Use as needed. Do not refrigerate this mixture.

Coffee cream icing

Beat the butter and sugar together as directed above and add 2 tablespoons of Camp coffee or strong fresh espresso instead of the chocolate. Add the milk, if necessary, to obtain a spreading consistency. Use to top the coffee and walnut sponge. Decorate with walnut halves.

Vanilla buttercream

Beat the butter and sugar together as above and add 1 teaspoon of vanilla extract instead of the chocolate.

Pound Cake

SERVES 10–12

1 rounded cup/9oz/250g butter, softened
1¼ cups/9oz/250g granulated (caster) sugar
zest of 1 lemon
5 medium eggs, lightly beaten

2¼ cups/9oz/250g all-purpose or plain flour
1 teaspoon baking powder
½ teaspoon salt
½ cup/4fl oz/120ml milk
confectioner's (icing) sugar, to decorate

Preheat the oven to 300° F/Gas 2/150° C.

❶ Lightly grease a non-stick kugelhopf tin or 12-cup bundt pan.

❷ Cream the butter and sugar together until light and fluffy. Beat in the lemon zest. Add the eggs, a little at a time, beating well after each addition. Gradually beat in the flour. Add the baking powder, salt, and milk and mix thoroughly. The mixture may appear curdled —this is okay. Pour into the prepared tin and level the surface. Bake in the center of the preheated oven for about 1 hour, 20 minutes or until risen and golden and a toothpick inserted into the middle comes out clean. Check after 1 hour, and if the top is very brown, cover loosely with a piece of aluminum foil.

❸ Let cool in the tin for 10 minutes, then turn on to a wire rack and let cool completely. Dust the cake lightly with confectioner's (icing) sugar, before serving cut into slices.

Chocolate Chip Cookies

MAKES ABOUT 24 COOKIES

1¹/₂ cups/6oz/175g all-purpose or plain flour
pinch of salt
1 teaspoon baking powder
¹/₄ teaspoon baking soda
¹/₃ cup/3oz/75g butter or margarine, plus extra for greasing

¹/₃ cup/2oz/50g light brown soft sugar
3 tablespoons golden syrup
1 tablespoon water or milk
¹/₂ cup/4oz/115g chocolate chips

Preheat the oven to 375° F/Gas 5/190° C.

❶ Lightly grease a large baking sheet.

❷ In a large bowl, sift together the flour, salt, baking powder, and baking soda.

❸ Cut the butter or margarine into small pieces and add to the flour mixture. Using two knives or your fingertips, rub in until the mixture resembles coarse breadcrumbs.

❹ Add the sugar, golden syrup, water, or milk and chocolate chips. Mix together until you have a smooth but firm dough.

❺ Shape the mixture into small balls and arrange well spaced on the baking sheet. Flatten slightly with the heel of your hand. Transfer to the oven and bake for 7–8 minutes until golden. Let cool slightly, then transfer the cookies to a wire rack.

❻ Alternatively, replace the chocolate chips with ³/₄ cup/4oz/115g of chopped hazelnuts.

Pumpkin and Nut Muffins with Brown Butter Icing

MAKES 12 MUFFINS

$^1/_2$ rounded cup/4$^1/_2$ oz/125g butter, softened

1$^1/_4$ cups/5oz/150g all-purpose or plain flour

$^3/_4$ cup/6oz/175g light brown soft sugar, lightly packed

1 cup/8oz/225g canned pumpkin or cooked pumpkin

1 large egg

2 teaspoons ground cinnamon

1 teaspoon vanilla extract

1 teaspoon baking powder

1 teaspoon baking soda

$^1/_2$ teaspoon ground nutmeg

$^3/_4$ cup/6fl oz/175ml milk

$^3/_4$ cup/4oz/125g whole-wheat flour

$^2/_3$ cup/3oz/75g pecans, roughly chopped

1 cup/3$^1/_2$ oz/100g raisins

FOR THE ICING

4 tablespoons/2oz/50g unsalted butter

1$^1/_2$ cups/8oz/225g confectioner's (icing) sugar

1$^1/_2$ teaspoons vanilla extract

2 tablespoons milk

Preheat the oven to 375° F/Gas 5/190° C.

❶ Lightly grease a 12-hole muffin pan or line with muffin papers.

❷ To make the muffins, using an electric whisk, beat the butter until fluffy. Add the flour, sugar, pumpkin, egg, cinnamon, vanilla extract, baking powder, baking soda, nutmeg, and milk. Beat until well combined, scraping down the sides of the bowl occasionally. Add the whole-wheat flour, pecans, and raisins and fold in until just combined.

❸ Fill the prepared pan until each hole is about two-thirds full. Transfer to the oven and bake for 25–30 minutes until risen and golden. Remove from the oven and let cool on a wire rack.

❹ To make the icing, melt the butter over a medium heat in a small saucepan until light golden brown. Remove from the heat and immediately add the confectioner's (icing) sugar, vanilla extract, and milk, stirring until smooth. Spread generously over the top of each cooled muffin.

Banana Bread

SERVES 8

⅓ cup/3oz/75g soft margarine
½ cup/4oz/115g granulated (caster) sugar
1 large egg, beaten
2 cups/8oz/225g/ all-purpose or plain flour
1 teaspoon baking powder

4 medium ripe bananas
zest of 1 orange
zest of 1 lemon
½ cup/2oz/50g walnuts, roughly chopped

Preheat the oven to 350° F/Gas 4/180° C.

❶ Grease and line the base of a 2lb/900g loaf pan. Set aside.

❷ Put the margarine, sugar, and egg in a large mixing bowl, then add the flour and baking powder. In another bowl, mash the bananas thoroughly.

❸ Using an electric whisk, beat the flour mixture until thoroughly combined before adding the orange and lemon zests, followed by the bananas and chopped walnuts. Mix together thoroughly and transfer to the prepared pan.

❹ Bake the cake in the center of the oven for 50–60 minutes until it is golden and risen. A skewer inserted in the middle of the cake

should come out clean. Let cool in the pan for 10 minutes before turning out onto a wire rack to cool completely.

❺ Serve in slices with butter. This cake actually improves in flavor if wrapped and kept overnight.

Banana, choc, and nut loaf

Substitute roughly chopped pecans for the walnuts in the above recipe and add ¼ cup/ 2oz/50g of chocolate chips. Bake as directed above.

Basic Shortcrust Pastry Recipe

MAKES 12OZ/350G PASTRY

2 cups/8oz/225g all-purpose or plain flour
pinch of salt

½ cup/4oz/115g butter, chilled
2–3 tablespoons cold water

❶ Sift the flour and salt into a large bowl. Dice the butter into ½in/1cm cubes and add to the flour. Rub the butter and flour together until the mixture resembles coarse breadcrumbs. Alternatively, put the flour and salt into a food processor with the butter. Process until the mixture resembles coarse breadcrumbs.

❷ Add 2 tablespoons of the water and, using a palette knife, mix the dough until it starts to form a ball—you may need to add all or some of the remaining water. Alternatively, add the water to the food processor and, using the pulse button, bring the dough together just until it forms a ball on the blade. You may need to add the remaining water.

❸ Turn the dough onto a floured surface and knead briefly until smooth. Form into a ball or a disc, wrap in plastic wrap (cling film) and refrigerate until needed.

Sweet shortcrust pastry

Add 2oz/50g granulated (caster) sugar to the mixture after the butter has been rubbed in. Continue as directed for Basic Shortcrust Pastry.

How do I rub the butter and flour together?

Add the fat to the flour and, using your fingertips, rub the two together to make the pieces of butter smaller and coated in the flour. Continue rubbing the two together until the mixture resembles coarse breadcrumbs. The butter pieces will be very small and the mixture will have changed color slightly, from white to pale yellow. It helps to have cold fingertips when you do this.

Puff Pastry (The Basic Method)

MAKES 12OZ/350G PASTRY

3 cups/12oz/350g all-purpose or plain flour
3/4 cup/6oz/175g unsalted butter
pinch of salt

2 egg yolks
6 tablespoons cold water

1 Put one quarter of the flour into a bowl with the butter. Using an electric mixer, combine the butter and flour thoroughly. Scrape the butter paste onto a sheet of plastic wrap (cling film), shape into a 5 x 6in/13 x 15cm rectangle, and leave it in a cool place (but not the refrigerator).

2 Put the remaining flour, egg yolks, water, and salt into a bowl and mix to a dough. If necessary, add a little more water, but the dough will soften on resting. Turn the dough onto a floured surface and knead for about 10 minutes until very smooth and elastic. Alternatively, put all the ingredients into the bowl of an electric mixer fitted with a dough hook and mix to dough. Knead for 6–7 minutes on a low speed.

3 Form the dough into a neat ball and wrap in plastic wrap. Rest in the refrigerator for at least 1 hour or overnight, if possible.

4 Lightly flour a work surface and roll out the dough to an 11in/28cm square. Place the rectangle of butter paste in the center and fold the corners of the dough over to completely enclose. Wrap in plastic wrap and chill for 30 minutes.

5 Place the dough on a lightly floured surface. Roll out the dough onto a 16 x 28in/41 x 71cm rectangle. Fold one end in by a sixth. Fold both ends until they meet in the center. Now fold the two together as if closing a book.

6 Turn the dough so that the fold is to one side. Roll the dough as before and fold one end in by a third, repeat at the other end to cover the first fold. Fold in half from left to right again as if closing a book. Brush off excess flour. This step is a single turn.

7 Place on a tray lined with plastic wrap and cover with more plastic wrap. Chill for 1 hour.

8 Put the dough on a floured surface so the fold is to one side. Roll again as before and give the dough a single turn (see step 6), followed by another. Wrap in plastic wrap and chill overnight before using.

Apple and Cinnamon Pie

SERVES 6-8

1 quantity sweet shortcrust pastry
(see page 118)
$^1/_4$–$^1/_3$ cup/2–3oz/50–75g granulated
(caster) sugar, plus extra for sprinkling

1 teaspoon ground cinnamon
2lb 4oz/1kg dessert apples
milk, for brushing

Preheat the oven to 400° F/Gas 6/200° C.

❶ Divide the pastry in two. On a lightly floured surface using a lightly floured rolling pin, roll one piece thinly to a 10in/25cm diameter circle and use to line a 9in/23cm pie dish. Mix together the sugar and cinnamon.

❷ Peel the apples, quarter lengthwise and core them. Slice the apples very thinly and add directly to the lined pie dish. After slicing each apple, sprinkle the slices with a little of the sugar and cinnamon. Do not worry if your apples lay higher than the lip of the pie dish.

❸ Roll out the remaining pastry to about a 10in/25cm diameter circle. Brush the edge

of the pastry in the pie dish with a little milk. Carefully lay the pastry over the apples and press down the edges to seal. Decorate with a fork, if desired. Trim off any excess pastry. Make a couple of slashes in the top of the pie, or prick with a fork a couple of times.

❹ Brush the top of the pastry with a little milk, then sprinkle with granulated (caster) sugar. Transfer to the center of the preheated oven and bake for 25–30 minutes until the pastry is golden and the apples tender. Serve warm or cold.

Help! Adding sugar has made the dough softer and a bit sticky.

This is normal when sugar is added. It means that the dough is less easy to use than ordinary shortcrust. However, it is also makes a crisper pastry that is well suited to dessert recipes.

Apple and raisin crumble

Preheat the oven to 400° F/Gas 6/200° C. Put 1½ cups/ 6oz/175g of all-purpose or plain flour in a large bowl with a pinch of salt. Add ½ cup/4oz/115g of diced, unsalted butter. Rub the flour and butter together until the mixture resembles coarse breadcrumbs—a few large lumps of butter are fine. Stir in ½ cup/2oz/50g of oats and ⅓ cup/3oz/75g of soft light brown sugar. Slice the apples as directed for the Apple and Cinnamon Pie and put them into an ovenproof dish. Mix in ¼ cup/2oz/50g of granulated (caster) sugar, 1 teaspoon of cinnamon and ½ cup/2oz/50g of raisins. Spoon over the flour mixture to cover the fruit evenly. Transfer to the preheated oven and cook for 25–30 minutes. Serve warm or cold with light (single) cream.

French apple tart

Preheat the oven to 400° F/Gas 6/200° C. Roll out a ½ quantity of shortcrust pastry, and use to line a 9in/23cm loose-bottomed tart pan. Rest in the refrigerator for 20 minutes, then line the pastry with baking parchment or foil. Fill the tart pan with baking beans or rice and bake for 10 minutes. Remove the paper or foil and beans or rice and return to the oven for a further 10–12 minutes or until golden and crisp. Remove from the oven and reduce the temperature to 350° F/Gas 4/180° C.

Mix together 3½oz/100g/½ cup of unsalted butter, ⅔ cup/3½ oz/100g of ground almonds, ½ cup/3½ oz/100g of granulated (caster) sugar, 1 tablespoon of all-purpose or plain flour and 1 egg to make a smooth paste. Spread this paste on the cooled pastry base. Peel, core, and thinly slice 2–3 dessert apples and lay in concentric circles on top of the almond paste. Bake for 50–60 minutes until the filling is risen and the apples are golden. Heat 2 tablespoons of apricot jam with 1 tablespoon of water in a small pan. Brush the warmed jam over the hot tart and let cool. Serve warm or cold.

Strawberry and Rhubarb Lattice Tart

SERVES 6–8

1¹⁄₂ quantity sweet shortcrust pastry
(see page 118)
4 cups/1lb/450g rhubarb, cut into chunks
¹⁄₃ –¹⁄₂ cup/3–4oz/75–115g granulated
(caster) sugar, to taste
zest of 1 orange

1¹⁄₂ tablespoons cornstarch (cornflour)
or arrowroot
2 cups/12oz/350g strawberries, hulled
and halved, if large
water or milk, for brushing
2 teaspoons raw brown (demerara) sugar

❶ Use about one third of the pastry to line a 9in/23cm loose-bottomed tart pan. Set aside in the refrigerator until needed along with the remaining pastry.

❷ Put the rhubarb, with ¹⁄₃ cup/3oz/75g of the sugar and the orange zest into a saucepan over a gentle heat. Cook, stirring occasionally, until the rhubarb is tender and quite juicy, but still holding its shape, about 8–10 minutes. Taste for sweetness and add the remaining sugar if necessary.

❸ Mix the cornstarch (cornflour) with about 1 tablespoon of cold water until smooth. Stir into the rhubarb, return the mixture to a gentle simmer and cook for about 1–2 minutes until thickened. Remove from the heat and leave until cold. Stir in the strawberries.

❹ Meanwhile, place a baking sheet on the center shelf of the oven and preheat to 400° F/Gas 6/200° C. Remove the pastry-lined pan from the refrigerator and line with foil or baking parchment. Fill with baking beans or rice and transfer to the oven. Cook for 12 minutes, then remove the foil or paper and beans. Return to the oven for a further 10 minutes until golden and crisp. Let cool slightly.

❺ Meanwhile, cut a large square of non-stick baking parchment and put on top of a large chopping board or flat plate. Make room in the freezer for this.

❻ Remove the excess pastry from the refrigerator. Then. on a lightly floured surface, roll the pastry out thinly to a large rectangle. Using a fluted pastry wheel or knife, cut out 10–12 long strips of pastry each about 1in/2.5cm wide. On the prepared chopping board or flat plate, weave the strips of pastry into a lattice pattern, leaving about ¹⁄₂in/1cm gap between the strips. When you have finished, transfer the board or plate to the freezer for about 20–30 minutes. This will make it very easy to transfer to the filled tart pan.

What is blind baking?

This is a term for cooking pastry in a tart pan before it is filled, which prevents the bottom of the pastry becoming soggy. The uncooked pastry is first lined with baking parchment or foil. It is then filled with baking beans or rice. The pastry is partially baked in the oven, then the beans and baking parchments are removed before the baking time is over to allow the pastry to brown.

7 Add the rhubarb-strawberry mixture to the cooked pastry case. Brush the edges of the pastry with a little water or milk. Remove the lattice top from the freezer. Transfer it to cover the filling. Cut off any excess from the edges using the fluted pastry wheel and press the pastry to seal the edges all round.

8 Brush the pastry lightly with a little water and sprinkle with the raw brown (demerara) sugar. Transfer the tart pan to the baking sheet in the oven and bake for 30–35 minutes until the pastry is golden

and the filling is bubbling. Let cool for about 15 minutes in the pan, carefully remove from the pan and let cool for an additional 10 minutes before serving cut into wedges. Also delicious served cold.

Desserts

A good dessert is the crowning glory of a fine meal. Often all you need are some perfectly ripe strawberries with a little light (single) cream. But an extravagant pudding or rich chocolate mousse can hardly be beaten. As with all cookery, a few well-chosen, good quality ingredients are the key to success.

Fruit

Fresh fruit is always a good basis for dessert. Look for firm, well-colored specimens with no soft spots or blemishes. Some fruit, such as peaches, nectarines, and pears, will benefit from ripening. In this case, keep them in a bowl at room temperature, perhaps with a ripe banana, which will help the process.

Cream

Generally speaking, the higher the fat content, the easier a cream will be to whip.

Light, single, or pouring cream will not hold its shape when whipped and so is best served as an accompaniment. It will also not stand being heated.

Whipping cream has a suitable fat content for whipping. Make sure the bowl and whisk are cold beforehand to make the job easier. Whipping cream is good for making ice cream, especially in an ice cream machine, since heavier cream can become granular.

Heavy or double cream has the highest fat content and whips up very easily. It is excellent for folding into mousses and mixtures that need to set. It is also resistant to splitting when heated and so it is good for cooking.

Soured cream and crème fraîche have a similar, slightly acidic flavor, and make excellent accompaniments to fruit desserts.

Chocolate

Chocolate comes in three main types:

Milk chocolate has, as the name suggests, extra milk solids added to it to give a creamy flavor. Look for milk chocolate that has cocoa solids of 40 per cent to use in cooking. Although it is less suited to cooking, as the flavor is not so pronounced and is prone to overheating, it is useful for decorating desserts and for making confectionery.

Semisweet, plain or dark chocolate is darker in color than milk chocolate, and has no added milk solids, and less added sugar. Look for plain chocolate with a high percentage of cocoa solids—good quality chocolate will range between 50–75 per cent, with the higher percentage being the most bitter. This chocolate has a wide range of uses, from cakes to mousses and truffles.

White chocolate has no cocoa solids, but is made using cocoa butter. Good quality brands will sometimes have added vanilla flavoring and all will have added sugar. White chocolate is the most difficult to cook with as it melts at a lower temperature and is therefore easier to overheat.

When making desserts, bear in mind that too much sugar will spoil the flavor. Always start with a smaller amount then add more to taste.

Custard

MAKES 2½ CUPS/1 PINT/600ML

1¼ cups/10fl oz/300ml milk
1¼ cups/10fl oz/300ml heavy
(double) cream
1 vanilla pod, split lengthwise or 1 teaspoon
vanilla extract

5 egg yolks
½ cup/3½ oz/100g granulated
(caster) sugar

❶ Put the milk, cream, and vanilla pod into a saucepan and bring slowly up to boiling point, stirring often. Immediately remove from the heat and let infuse for 15 minutes.

❷ Meanwhile, whisk the egg yolks and sugar until thick and pale. Remove the vanilla pod and pour the milk and cream mixture onto the egg and sugar, whisking all the time.

❸ Return this mixture to a clean saucepan and place over a low heat. Stirring constantly with a wooden spoon, cook over a gentle heat until thickened. Do not allow to boil or the egg will scramble. The custard is ready when the mixture coats the back of a wooden spoon without running off freely.

❹ Serve warm or cold. Do not freeze.

Help my custard is curdling!

To stabilize your custard, add 2 teaspoons of cornstarch (cornflour) to the egg yolks and sugar. If the custard should come to the boil and start to curdle, immediately transfer the mixture to a large mixing bowl and whisk until smooth.

Anyone for custard?

Hot Chocolate Sauce

MAKES 2 CUPS/¾ PINT/450ML

¾ cup/4oz/115g semisweet, plain, or dark chocolate, chopped

1¼ cups/10fl oz/300ml heavy (double) cream

❶ Put the chocolate into a heatproof bowl. In a saucepan, bring the cream up to boiling point, remove from the heat and leave for a minute to allow it to come off the boil. Pour the cream over the chocolate. Let stand for about 1 minute, then stir until smooth. Use immediately as needed.

❷ If left to go cold, the chocolate sauce will set. To reheat, put the heatproof bowl over a pan of simmering water. Do not allow the bottom of the bowl to touch the water. Leave the sauce without stirring until melted. Stir to mix and use.

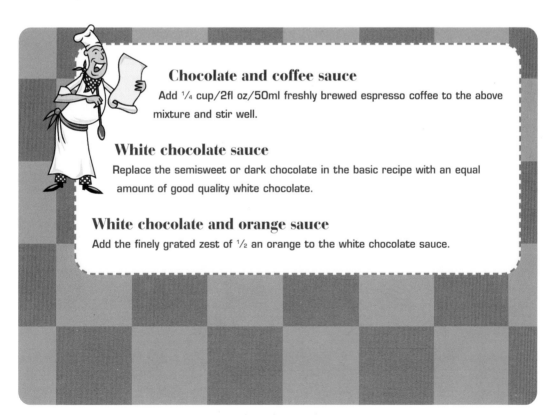

Chocolate and coffee sauce

Add ¼ cup/2fl oz/50ml freshly brewed espresso coffee to the above mixture and stir well.

White chocolate sauce

Replace the semisweet or dark chocolate in the basic recipe with an equal amount of good quality white chocolate.

White chocolate and orange sauce

Add the finely grated zest of ½ an orange to the white chocolate sauce.

Rich Vanilla Ice Cream

MAKES 3 CUPS/1¼ PINTS/750ML

1¼ cups/10fl oz/300ml milk
1 vanilla pod, split lengthwise or 1
teaspoon vanilla extract
5 egg yolks

½ cup/3½ oz/100g granulated
(caster) sugar
1¼ cups/10fl oz/300ml heavy
(double) cream

❶ Make the custard as described on page 128, but do not add the cream. When the custard has cooled, refrigerate until chilled.

❷ Whisk the cream until soft peaks form, then fold into the chilled custard. Pour this mixture into a freezerproof container—a shallow rectangular box with a lid is ideal.

❸ Cover and freeze for 2 hours. Remove from the freezer and beat the mixture using an electric

or balloon whisk until smooth. Repeat freezing and whisking twice, then freeze until firm. The whisking during freezing prevents large ice crystals from forming and ensures that the ice cream is smooth.

❹ Alternatively, use an ice cream machine, following the manufacturer's instructions.

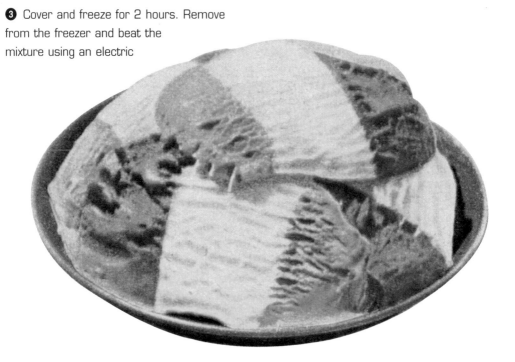

Chocolate ice cream

Follow the recipe for Vanilla Ice Cream on page 130, but add ³/₄ cup/4oz/115g of melted semisweet or plain chocolate to the custard once it is cooked.

Caramel ice cream

Using the ingredients and quantities for Vanilla Ice Cream on page 130, melt the sugar in a heavy-based pan with about 3 tablespoons of water. As soon as the sugar has dissolved, increase the heat and boil until the sugar turns a very dark golden color—it is important to be bold here, or the ice cream will be too sweet. Carefully swirl the pan if the sugar isn't coloring evenly. As soon as it is a dark mahogany color, remove from the heat, wait a minute or two, then pour on the cream, standing well back so you don't get splattered. When the bubbling subsides, stir until smooth.

Meanwhile, put the vanilla pod into a saucepan with the milk and bring up to the boil, as before. Let infuse. Beat the egg yolks until pale, then pour over the milk, discarding the vanilla pod. Return this mixture to a fresh saucepan and cook as described. When cooked, add to the caramel and cream mixture, stirring until well blended. Freeze as directed.

Berry-flavored ices

Berry-flavored ices are very easy. Put 4 cups/1lb 2oz/500g of washed and hulled berries (strawberries or raspberries work very well) into a food processor with ¹/₂ cup/3¹/₂ oz/100g of granulated (caster) sugar and the juice of 1 lemon. Process until smooth. If you want to remove the seeds, press this mixture through a sieve. Otherwise, put into a bowl and add 1¹/₄ cups/10fl oz/300ml of whipping cream and stir well. Transfer to a freezerproof container and follow the freezing instructions for Vanilla Ice Cream.

Chocolate Mousse

SERVES 8

7oz/200g semisweet or plain chocolate, 50 per cent cocoa solids

4 eggs, separated

³/₄ cup/6fl oz/175ml heavy (double) cream, plus extra to serve

❶ Break the semisweet or plain chocolate into pieces in a small, heatproof bowl. Put the bowl over a pan of barely simmering water, ensuring that the bowl doesn't touch the water, and leave without stirring until the chocolate has melted. Remove from the heat and let cool for a few minutes.

❷ Add 4 egg yolks and beat into the chocolate—it will thicken the mixture but not stiffen. If the mixture is dry-looking and stiff, the chocolate has been over-heated and you will need to start again.

❸ Leave the chocolate mixture to cool for about 15 minutes.

❹ Whisk the heavy (double) cream until it holds soft peaks. Fold this into the chocolate.

❺ Whisk 4 egg whites until they hold soft peaks and fold into the chocolate mixture.

❻ Spoon into eight small serving dishes, cover with plastic wrap (clingfilm) and refrigerate for about 2 hours before serving, with a little extra cream if desired.

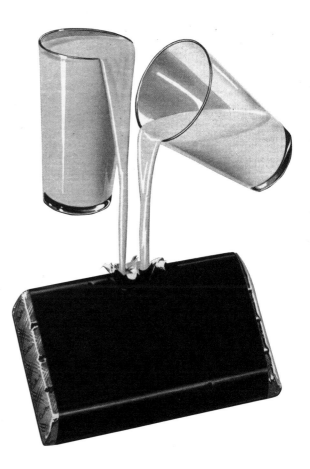

Strawberry Cheesecake

SERVES 10-12

FOR THE BASE

3 cups/8oz/225g graham crackers (digestive biscuits), finely crushed

4 tablespoons/2oz/50g butter, melted

¼ cup/2oz/50g candied peel, very finely chopped *(optional)*

FOR THE FILLING

2¼ cups/1lb 5oz/600g full fat cream cheese

¾ cup/6oz/175g granulated (caster) sugar

1 teaspoon vanilla extract

1¼ cups/10fl oz/300ml whipping cream, whipped to soft peaks

FOR THE TOPPING

4 cups/1lb 2oz/500g strawberries, hulled

2–3 tablespoons confectioner's (icing) sugar, to taste

juice of ½ lemon

❶ To make the base, lightly oil an 8in/20cm springform pan. Mix the cracker crumbs with the melted butter and candied peel, if using. Spread in an even layer over the bottom of the pan and press down well. Refrigerate while you make the filling.

❷ To make the filling, beat the cheese and sugar with the vanilla extract until smooth. Carefully fold in the whipped cream, taking care not to overbeat or the mixture will separate. Spread this mixture on top of the biscuit base and level the surface. Refrigerate for at least 4 hours, preferably overnight.

❸ To make the topping, put 5oz/150g/ 1 cup of the strawberries into a food processor along with the confectioner's (icing) sugar, and lemon juice. Blend to a purée. Press through a sieve to remove the seeds. Halve the remaining strawberries and put into a bowl with the puréed strawberries. Mix together. Taste and add more confectioner's (icing) sugar if necessary.

❹ To serve, loosen the pan and remove the outer ring and put onto a large serving plate. Spoon the strawberry purée over the top, allowing a little to run down the sides. Top with the remaining strawberries and cut into small wedges (it's very rich) and serve.

Lemon Surprise Pudding

SERVES 4

4 tablespoons/2oz/50g butter, softened, plus extra for greasing
heaped ½ cup/4oz/120g granulated (caster) sugar

finely grated zest and juice of 2 large lemons
2 eggs, separated
½ cup/2oz/50g self-rising flour
¾ cup/6fl oz/175ml milk

Preheat the oven to 350° F/Gas 4/180° C.

❶ Butter a 3¾ cups/1½ pint/900ml pudding basin or baking dish and set aside.

❷ Beat the butter, sugar, and lemon zest together until well mixed. Next beat in the egg yolks, a little at a time. Fold in the flour, alternating with the milk and lemon juice. Finally, whisk the egg whites and fold them into the mixture. At this stage, the mixture will look curdled, but this is to be expected.

❸ Pour the mixture into the prepared pudding basin or baking dish and bake in the center of the oven for 40–45 minutes until golden brown and risen.

❹ Serve hot with pouring cream.

Spiced Baked Apples

SERVES 4

6 large dessert apples
6 tablespoons/3oz/75g unsalted butter,
softened
$^1/_4$ cup/2oz/50g light brown soft sugar
$^1/_2$ cup/1$^1/_2$ oz/40g fresh
white breadcrumbs
1 green cardamom pod
$^1/_2$ teaspoon ground cinnamon

$^1/_4$ teaspoon freshly grated nutmeg
pinch of saffron strands
finely grated zest of $^1/_2$ lemon
$^1/_4$ cup/1oz/25g sultanas
$^1/_8$ cup/1oz/25g shelled and
chopped pistachios
1$^1/_4$ cups/10fl oz/300ml dry cider

Preheat the oven to 400° F/Gas 6/200° C.

❶ Core the apples leaving them whole. Using a small sharp knife, make a horizontal cut around the middle of the apples—this will prevent the skin from bursting during cooking.

❷ In a medium mixing bowl, cream together the butter, sugar, and breadcrumbs. Crush the cardamom pods and remove the black seeds. Crush these using a mortar and pestle or with the back of a spoon. Add to the butter mixture along with the cinnamon, nutmeg, saffron, and lemon zest. Mix everything together well. Stir in the sultanas and pistachios.

❸ Divide this mixture between the six apples, stuffing it down tightly into where the cores used to be and piling any excess mixture on top of the apples. Transfer the apples to a ceramic or glass ovenproof dish large enough to hold them all with a little space in between. Pour the cider around the apples.

❹ Transfer the dish to the preheated oven and bake for about 40–45 minutes until the apples are very tender.

❺ Serve warm with the juices from the baking dish and some cold pouring cream.

Orange Terrine with Citrus Cream

5 large oranges
2¹/₂ cups/1 pint/600ml fresh orange juice
¹/₄ cup/2oz/50g granulated (caster) sugar
6 sheets leaf gelatine

FOR THE CITRUS CREAM
2 tablespoons confectioner's (icing) sugar
1¹/₄ cups/10fl oz/300ml whipping cream
1 tablespoon orange flower water
grated zest and juice of 1 lemon
grated zest of 1 lime

❶ Top and tail each orange with a serrated fruit knife. Stand on one flat end and, following the curve of the orange, cut down the sides to remove the peel.

❷ Hold the orange in one hand and carefully cut down in between the membranes, releasing the segments, which should now be clean and clear of any membranes.

❸ Put the fresh orange juice and granulated (caster) sugar in a saucepan and heat to nearly boiling, allowing the sugar to dissolve. Remove from the heat.

❹ Add the gelatine to the heated orange juice mixture and stir until dissolved. Let cool.

❺ Lightly oil a 5 cups/2 pint/1.2 liter capacity terrine mold and place a layer of orange segments across the bottom. Continue to layer until three-quarters full. Pour the orange juice in and allow to set in the refrigerator for at least 6 hours. Turn out onto a flat serving plate.

❻ For the citrus cream, just before serving sift the confectioner's (icing) sugar into the cream, add the orange flower water, and whip until it holds soft peaks. Stir in the lemon and lime zest, and the lemon juice. Serve with the terrine.

Chocolate Espresso Pots

SERVES 8

6oz/175g semisweet or plain chocolate, 70 per cent cocoa solids, plus a little extra for decorating
1¼ cups/10fl oz/300ml strong, fresh espresso coffee

2 tablespoons coffee liqueur or whisky
¼ cup/2oz/50g granulated (caster) sugar
6 egg yolks
¼ cup/2fl oz/50ml heavy (double) cream, to serve

❶ Break the semisweet or plain chocolate into pieces and put into a heatproof bowl along with the coffee and coffee liqueur. Set the bowl over a pan of simmering water. The bowl should not touch the water. Leave, without stirring, until the chocolate has melted, then stir until smooth. Remove from the heat and stir in the sugar. Let cool for about 5 minutes.

❷ Beat in the egg yolks, then pour the mixture through a sieve into eight small espresso cups or ramekins. Let cool, then refrigerate for at least 4 hours, or overnight.

❸ When ready to serve, lightly whip the cream and put a spoonful on top of each chocolate cup. Sprinkle over a little extra grated chocolate and serve.

Why boil chocolate over water?

Chocolate is very heat-sensitive and can burn easily—especially when it is melted alone. To combat this chocolate should always be heated in a heatproof bowl over a pan of simmering water so that the heat is not directly on the chocolate. Place half of the chocolate in the heatproof bowl. Begin to stir the chocolate with a spatula only when the outside edges of the chocolate begin to melt. Gradually add the rest of the chocolate. When it has almost melted remove the bowl from the heat, and continue stirring until the chocolate is smooth and shiny.

Banana Toffee Cheesecake

SERVES 10-12

FOR THE PASTRY

scant 1 cup/8oz/225g all-purpose or
plain flour
pinch salt
¹/₂ cup/4oz/115g butter, diced
¹/₄ cup/2oz/50g granulated (caster) sugar
3–4 tablespoons cold water

FOR THE FILLING

4oz/115g semisweet or plain chocolate,
plus extra for decoration
14oz/400g can sweetened condensed milk
1 cup/9oz/250g mascarpone cheese
²/₃ cup/5fl oz/150ml heavy (double) cream,
lightly whipped
3 large ripe but firm bananas
juice of ¹/₂ lemon

Preheat the oven to 400° F/gas 6/200° C.

❶ Follow steps 1, 2, and 3 in the basic
Shortcrust Pastry method (see page 118),
stirring the sugar into the rubbed in mixture
before kneading and chilling.

❷ Roll the pastry into a large circle on a
lightly floured surface, about 2in/5cm larger
than a 9in/23cm plain pastry ring, and place
on a baking sheet. Ease the pastry into the
ring. Line the pastry case with foil or baking
parchment and fill with baking beans.

❸ Transfer the pastry to the oven and bake
for 12 minutes. Remove the baking beans and
foil and cook for 10–12 minutes until golden.
Remove from the oven and set aside to cool.
Brush off any crumbs from inside the case.

❹ To make the filling, break the chocolate
into pieces and melt it in a bowl over a pan of
simmering water. Do not let the bowl touch
the water. Using a pastry brush, paint the
chocolate onto the pastry case to cover
completely. Chill until set.

❺ Put the can of condensed milk into a deep
pan and cover with water by at least 2in/5cm.
Bring to the boil and simmer for 4 hours,
topping up with water as necessary. Keep the
can completely submerged at all times.
Remove the pan from the heat and leave the
can until it is completely cold before opening.

❻ To assemble the cheesecake, thickly slice
the bananas and drizzle with the lemon juice.
Beat the mascarpone cheese until softened,
then stir in the cream. Carefully fold the
cream mixture and toffee together but don't
overmix—leave them marbled. Fold in the
bananas, then spoon into the pastry case.
Grate the extra chocolate over the top.

Index

Picture Credits